The Numerology Guidebook

ALSO BY MICHELLE BUCHANAN

NUMEROLOGY GUIDANCE CARDS (44-card deck and guidebook)

Please visit:

Hay House USA: www.hayhouse.com®
Hay House Australia: www.hayhouse.com.au
Hay House UK: www.hayhouse.co.uk
Hay House South Africa: www.hayhouse.co.za
Hay House India: www.hayhouse.co.in

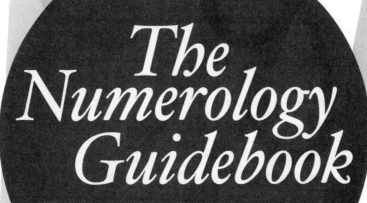

The Numerology Guidebook

Uncover Your Destiny and the Blueprint of Your Life

Michelle Buchanan

HAY HOUSE, INC.
Carlsbad, California • New York City
London • Sydney • Johannesburg
Vancouver • Hong Kong • New Delhi

Published and distributed in the United States by: Hay House, Inc.: www .hayhouse.com® • *Published and distributed in Australia by:* Hay House Australia Pty. Ltd.: www.hayhouse.com.au • *Published and distributed in the United Kingdom by:* Hay House UK, Ltd.: www.hayhouse.co.uk • *Published and distributed in the Republic of South Africa by:* Hay House SA (Pty), Ltd.: www.hayhouse. co.za • *Distributed in Canada by:* Raincoast: www.raincoast.com • *Published in India by:* Hay House Publishers India: www.hayhouse.co.in

Cover design: stevenwilliams.org.uk • *Interior design:* Tricia Breidenthal

Library of Congress Cataloging-in-Publication Data

Buchanan, Michelle.
  The numerology guidebook : uncover your destiny and the blueprint of your life / Michelle Buchanan. -- 1st edition.
     pages cm
  ISBN 978-1-4019-4359-2 (tradepaper : alk. paper) 1. Numerology. I. Title.
  BF1623.P9B73 2013
  133.3'35--dc23

                                    2013023636

Tradepaper ISBN: 978-1-4019-4359-2

16 15 14 13   4 3 2 1
1st edition, December 2013

Printed in the United States of America

To Ben and Ava.
If Mommy can make her dreams come true,
then so can you!
Always follow your dreams and never stop believing!
Mommy loves you both—big-time!

This book is dedicated to everyone with a dream—
keep on believing.

CONTENTS

PART II: Forecasting and Timing

PART III: Other Numbers in Your Life

PREFACE

If everybody knew their "numbers," the world would be a better place.

The reason I'm so passionate about numerology is that it truly changed *my* life! After struggling for many years to make sense of myself and my experiences, it was a numerology reading from a stranger that turned my life around. I couldn't believe that someone I didn't even know could discern so much about me and the challenges I faced simply by calculating the numbers in my date of birth and birth-certificate name. To say it was a life-changing experience is an understatement. That 40-minute reading taught me more about myself than ten years' worth of therapy with the best therapist in the world.

Thanks to numerology, for the first time in my life I was able to understand who I was and why I'd struggled with an eating disorder, addiction, and other self-destructive behavior. After years of crippling anxiety and self-doubt, I was finally able to process my thoughts, emotions, and fears, and understand the reasons why my life had unfolded the way it had. From the moment I discovered that my personality traits and life experiences were typical of my numbers, something within me changed. And that acknowledgment alone enabled me to take full responsibility for my life and begin my long and progressive journey toward self-love and understanding—a journey that might not have begun at all if I hadn't discovered my numbers.

Ever since that day over 20 years ago, I've been on a crusade to learn everything I can about numerology so I can fully understand myself and discover my life purpose. I started out by reading every numerology book I could get my hands on. I purchased some from metaphysical bookstores, borrowed others from the library, and ordered still more from overseas. For once in my life, my obsessive nature had come in handy and was working to my advantage.

From 1997 to 1999, I took numerology night classes with New Zealand's most experienced numerologist, the late Francie Williams, at the North Shore Parapsychology School while working in my corporate sales job during the day. However, despite my ability to provide accurate and inspirational readings for my corporate clients, family, friends, and countless others who crossed my path, I lacked the necessary self-esteem to charge money for my wisdom and time.

At 39 I became a stay-at-home mom with my second child. During this time I took an in-depth Law of Attraction practitioners course that enabled me to recognize the two limiting beliefs that prevented me from charging a fee for my readings and making numerology my career. Those debilitating beliefs were: *I'm not good enough to accept money for my knowledge and time* and *People only want psychic and clairvoyant readings—there isn't a market for numerology.*

Once I changed my outlook and reprogrammed my limiting beliefs, I was able to fully embrace my life purpose as an Inspirational Teacher (according to my 11/2 Life Path and 11/2 Soul numbers) and take steps toward making numerology my career. Today, I'm living my dream as a full-time numerologist with clients all over the world. I'm honored to say that I am living proof that when you change your thoughts and follow your numerology blueprint, you can make your dreams come true.

✳

Because numerology has had such a positive impact on my life, I'm driven to help others find happiness, too, by helping them recognize the influence of their numbers. As far as I'm concerned, numerology is the fast-track way to self-love and empowerment. It's one of most valuable tools available to help improve your quality of life. I feel very strongly about this because I know from personal experience that *numerology leads to self-understanding, self-understanding leads to self-acceptance, self-acceptance leads to self-love, and self-love leads to empowerment.* When you feel fully empowered and have unconditional love for yourself, you *will* have a better life . . . because it's universal law!

When you know who you are; why you're here; where you're going; and why you think, feel, and behave the way you do, you're able to stand in your full power, which raises your energy vibration and enables you to better the circumstances of your life. Did you know that self-love is one of the key ingredients for the successful manifestation of your dreams? And did you know that *lack* of self-love is one of the primary causes of unhappiness and disease? To me, numerology is about so much more than simply predicting the future or choosing the ideal partner, wedding date, or name. It's the missing piece of the puzzle that will help you live your best life and reach your full potential.

I can almost guarantee that by the time you finish this book, you'll be well on your way toward unconditional self-love, as well as creating an overall better quality of life. As you read through these pages, you'll realize that you only face the challenges you do because they are your *numerological life lessons*—lessons you've "prechosen" and have the ability to overcome! As you calculate your numbers, you'll uncover your life's blueprint and the predetermined destiny that will help you actualize your dreams. I believe that this newfound insight into your soul's journey will enhance your appreciation for yourself and the life you've chosen to live.

I recommend you read this book cover to cover to obtain a complete understanding of numerology so you can fully benefit from its wisdom:

— As you read through the descriptions of the 7 Core Numbers in **Part I**, you will not only uncover your destiny, life purpose, strengths, weaknesses, and life lessons, you'll discover the astrological equivalent for each of your numbers, along with suitable career choices and the numbers of the people you are most compatible with.

— And the fun doesn't stop there! In **Part II**, "Forecasting and Timing," you'll learn how to calculate your various life cycles so you can determine what lies ahead. By knowing what's around the corner, you can prepare yourself for potential challenges and take advantage of the opportunities coming your way.

— By the time you reach **Part III**, "Other Numbers in Your Life," you'll be astounded by the numbers all around you and the influence they have on many areas of your life. I bet you didn't think that the numbers corresponding to the name of your business, your street, or even your house could have an effect on the circumstances of your life! Well, they *do,* and this section will explain how. This is one of my favorite areas of the book because the "Manifestation with Numbers" segment teaches you how you can use your numbers to your advantage, to manifest your dreams. And not only that, this section will teach you everything you need to know about changing and choosing a name. Whether it's selecting a business or pet name or determining whether to adopt a different name after marriage or divorce, this section will show you how to make the best decisions for *you.*

By the time you finish this book, you will see that your numerological life purpose isn't something you *do* or something you *achieve*—rather, it is something you *become.* I wrote this book to show you that fulfilling your life purpose is surrendering to the inherent energy that already resides within you and enables you to become your true authentic self. When you fully align with the numerological essence of all you are, you will reach your full potential and experience inner peace.

Your life purpose has nothing to do with how much money you have, what you do for a living, your physical appearance, or what you have or haven't accomplished. This book will show you that you're exactly as you are meant to be and are already on the right path! So grab a calculator and a pen, and plenty of scrap paper to calculate your numbers . . . and prepare to uncover your destiny and the blueprint of your life. Once you've witnessed your potential, your life will never be the same—because it's onward and upward from here.

From the bottom of my heart, I thank you for reading *The Numerology Guidebook*. I hope you enjoy reading it as much as I enjoyed writing it for you. And most of all, I hope that numerology will improve your life as much as it has improved mine.

Love and blessings,
Michelle

INTRODUCTION

What Is Numerology?

Numerology is the ancient science of numbers, with each number contributing a unique vibration to the story of your life. One of the benefits of numerology is that it can uncover your destiny and life purpose and the life lessons you'll face along the way, which is valuable information if you want to make the most of your journey. Even though this is one of the most accurate and powerful self-help tools available today, it originally dates back thousands of years to the ancient civilizations of Atlantis, Babylon, China, Egypt, India, and Greece.

These days, *Western* (aka modern) numerology is the most popular system used around the world. It is said to have been created by Pythagoras, the Greek mystic and mathematician, more than 2,500 years ago; however, some believe that the Western system wasn't actually developed until after his death. Even though Pythagoras is considered the father of modern numerology, the *Chaldean* system of numerology (developed by the Chaldeans of ancient Babylon) dates back even further. Besides Western and Chaldean, other numerology systems currently being used around the world today include the Kabbalistic, Chinese, and Tamil/Indian.

Numerology is based on the premise that we are timeless souls who have lived, and will continue to live, many lives for the purpose of wisdom and growth. We numerologists believe that every one of us, in our quest for self-mastery, has a preset agenda consisting of the specific lessons we'd like to learn and the destiny we endeavor to fulfill while we're here—the details of which are found in our numbers. In other words, we have prechosen our numbers prior to this incarnation to provide the necessary tools and experiences to assist us in our quest.

The Western numerology system used in this book will help you uncover the prechosen blueprint of your life using the numbers corresponding to your date of birth, birth-certificate name, and the name you currently use today. As you read through these pages, you'll discover that your life's mission is written in your numbers. The beauty of numerology is that it focuses on two main areas: *personality profiling* and *forecasting*. So not only will you determine your personality strengths and weaknesses, life lessons, destiny, and purpose, but you'll also uncover your future potential, the environment around you, and the direction in which your life is leading you.

※

Now before we get started, there are a couple of things I'd like to point out to make your learning experience easier. By taking the following into consideration, you will find it much easier to process the information in the book:

— **In numerology, a number has the same meaning wherever it appears.** So regardless of which system you use, once you understand the meaning of each number and what each chart position represents, it becomes a matter of mix and match.

— **The accuracy of a reading relies upon your ability to "blend" the numbers.** A numerology chart (profile of numbers) must be read in its entirety to get an accurate overall picture. This is where common sense and logic are just as important as intuition and insight.

— **Every number has positives and negatives.** So there's no such thing as a "good" or "bad" number, let alone the "perfect number" that guarantees a challenge-free life.

— **Every number has life lessons and challenges** to overcome so you can reach your full potential. Since you incarnated to learn and grow from your life experiences here on Earth, regardless of how *spiritual, well behaved, healthy, intelligent,* or *positive* you are, there will always be lessons to learn. Your attitude is the key to determining how challenging your lessons may be and how long your difficulties will last. The sooner you face your challenges head-on with courage, determination, optimism, and grace, the sooner you'll improve your quality of life.

— **For greater insight into a number, read** *every description* **for that number.** For example, if you're a 7 Life Path Number, read every 7 description such as those of the 7 Destiny Number, 7 Soul Number, 7 Karmic Lesson Number, 7 Pinnacle Number, and so on. Even though the *chart position* is different, the meaning is the same, because *a number has the same meaning wherever it appears.* To some extent, every description of that number will apply to you as well. You'll also gain additional information about that number that may not appear in your description.

— **Numbers, stars, and archetypes are complementary.** Certain astrology signs and archetypes have personality traits that are similar to the numbers. If you have the personality traits of a number, but that number doesn't appear in your chart, you may have its astrological or archetypal equivalent. For example, the monk archetype has similar personality traits to number 7, and the astrology sign Gemini has similar traits to number 5. (For further information about archetypes, I strongly recommend Caroline Myss's book *Archetypes: A Beginner's Guide to Your Inner-net.* For more information about astrology, check out *Linda Goodman's Sun Signs.*)

— Along with all forms of divination, numerology is only a guide. It cannot predict everything, and it cannot be 100 percent correct. So use your common sense, and take it all with a grain of salt.

— Conflicting theories among numerologists can be confusing for numerology students. When one numerologist says one thing and another says the opposite, it's hard to know which theory is "right." However, neither is right or wrong, just different. Each numerologist is simply teaching his or her own interpretation and preferred method of calculation. For example, some people prefer to make a chocolate cake with butter, and others prefer oil. In this book, I've tried my best to cover the various interpretations, systems, and calculation methods available so you can decide for yourself which ones work for you—because at the end of the day, it comes down to personal preference.

While we're on the subject, let me quickly address a couple of conflicting theories, as well as some other frequently asked questions, to clear up any confusion. . . .

Which numerology system is best— Western or Chaldean?

I adore both, but one is not better or more accurate than the other—they're just two completely different systems. There are many major differences between the two; however, the main ones are that Chaldean is an older system based on a letters-and-numbers chart where the numbers range from 1 to 8. Because the Chaldeans considered 9 a holy number, it isn't included in their letters-and-numbers chart.

In Chaldean numerology, the numerical value of each letter is based upon its sound frequency and vibrational pattern, whereas the value of each letter in the Western letters-and-numbers chart is based upon its position in the alphabet. As you can see on the next page, in Western numerology the numbers in the letters-and-numbers chart range from 1 to 9.

Another point of difference is that the letter *Y* is always considered a vowel in Chaldean numerology, but it can either be a consonant or a vowel in Western. Some Chaldean numerologists also place a greater significance on the name currently used today if it differs from the original birth-certificate name due to marriage, adoption, or other means, whereas Western often focuses predominantly on the original birth-certificate name.

Even though the definitions of the numbers themselves are the same for both systems, the chart positions in a numerology profile have different titles and meanings. For example, the total of the birth date is called the *Life Path Number* in Western but is called the *Destiny Number* in Chaldean, and each has a different meaning. I suggest you explore both systems (along with the many variations therein) to determine which is the most suitable for you.

Chaldean Letters-and-Numbers Chart

1	2	3	4	5	6	7	8
A	B	C	D	E	U	O	F
I	K	G	M	H	V	Z	P
J	R	L	T	N	W		
Q		S		X			
Y							

Miriam Roberts

Western Letters-and-Numbers Chart

1	2	3	4	5	6	7	8	9
A	B	C	D	E	F	G	H	I
J	K	L	M	N	O	P	Q	R
S	T	U	V	W	X	Y	Z	

Miriam Roberts

Is it necessary to know the time and place of birth to calculate a numerology chart?

No, this is only a requirement for astrology. In numerology, all you need is the date of birth; the full, original birth-certificate name; and the first and last name you currently go by today. It's essential that this information be 100 percent correct; otherwise the entire reading will be wrong. Therefore, it is wise to double-check the spelling on your birth certificate before calculating your numbers. It also pays to confirm the details of others before taking the time to calculate their numbers. Guesswork doesn't cut it in the world of numerology.

Should the birth-certificate name or current name be used to calculate a chart?

Both must be used to uncover a complete and accurate story of one's life; however, Western numerology places a greater emphasis on the original birth-certificate name, because it reveals the prechosen destiny that cannot be replaced by a new name. Most Chaldean numerologists believe the name currently used today (if it differs from the original birth-certificate name) carries the strongest vibration of all. No wonder people get confused! Either way, we'll be covering both names in this book.

Does a 3" × 3" grid, as seen in some numerology books, have to be used to calculate a numerology chart?

The square grid is called the *Pythagorean Birth Chart Grid* or the *Lo Shu Square,* and even though it's incredibly insightful, it isn't necessary that you use one in order to give a thorough and accurate reading. Whether you choose to use the grid or not comes down to personal preference.

If my numbers are incompatible with my partner's, will the relationship fail?

Not necessarily, so try not to get caught up in a "numbers compatibility" thing. There are so many components to take into consideration that it's impossible for any relationship to tick all the boxes. Other things to consider are:

- **The "complete" numerology chart.** For example, if the Life Path Numbers are considered incompatible, other numbers in the chart (such as the Soul and Destiny Numbers) may be compatible—or one person's Life Path Number may be compatible with the other person's Destiny Number.

- **The two individuals' astrology profiles.** While a couple's numbers may be considered incompatible, their astrology profiles may be compatible.

- **Soul contracts** (that is, prechosen agreements, made between souls prior to incarnation, to share specific life experiences together for the purpose of soul growth).

- **The fact that opposites often attract** when partners have specific lessons to learn from each other or need to adopt opposing personality traits.

I have clients with so-called incompatible numbers who've been happily married for years. Besides, numerologists have conflicting opinions about compatible numbers anyway. This is why

I use the phrase *are said to be most compatible with* when providing the so-called most compatible numbers.

Can numerology predict winning lottery numbers and a person's day of passing?

No, but it would be handy if it could! However, nothing can predict either of those things.

Is there such a thing as a lucky number?

No. It's your power of belief that makes a number—or anything else, for that matter—lucky. Since *what you believe to be will be,* if you believe a number is lucky or unlucky, then it *will* be.

Upon entering my birth date and name, I was urged by a numerology website to purchase one of their numerology reports, stating there was a "life-changing event" on the horizon. Is this for real or a scam?

Sadly, it's a scam. Please use your common sense when visiting these types of websites and walk away from anything that uses scare tactics, glitz and glamour, or a promise of fortune and fame to create a sale. Be mindful of fake testimonials, and research the website thoroughly to see if it has a good reputation before you spend your money. Otherwise, only deal with a reputable numerologist for authentic advice. Your local metaphysical store should be able to point you in the right direction. Failing that, most numerology authors (myself included) provide e-mail reports and Skype or telephone readings to people anywhere in the world. If you wish to receive a numerology service from me, please come directly to my website: www.michellebuchanan.co.nz. (Any other website that advertises my image and name is a fake.)

When it comes to numerology, I suggest that you explore every option and evaluate your findings through personal experience before deciding which system and methods you prefer. By testing the calculations out on yourself, you can determine which theories suit you best. And if you ever get hung up on the many numerology terms to remember, feel free to refer to the handy Glossary at the back of the book for a refresher.

Now, with the housekeeping out the way, let's get to the good stuff and start working out your numbers.

✦ ✦ ✦

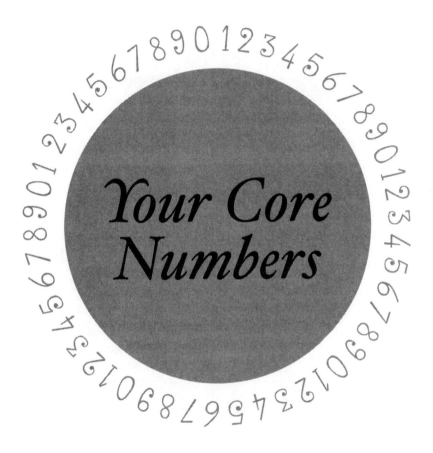

PART I

Your Core Numbers

Calculating Your Core Numbers

There are many numbers in a complete numerology chart; however, the seven numbers that have the most significance with respect to your personality and life's journey are the following:

- Life Path Number

- Destiny Number

- Soul Number

- Personality Number

- Maturity Number

- Birth Day Number

- Current Name Number

When compiling a numerology chart for yourself and others, it's important to "blend" the personality traits of each of the 7 Core Numbers above to get an accurate summary of the person as a whole. You can think of a numerology chart as a bowl of minestrone soup—it's the entire combination of ingredients that create the soup's flavor, rather than a single tomato (Life Path Number) or onion (Destiny Number). It's only when you take all of the numbers into consideration that you can see the complete story of someone's life.

In order to create an accurate personality profile, it also pays to take an individual's astrology chart into consideration. In fact, the astrology sign has a significant influence over the way people express themselves through their numbers. For example, an Aries 1 Life Path is a lot more headstrong, courageous, and pioneering, and will therefore have stronger leadership tendencies, than a sensitive and sympathetic Cancer 1 Life Path.

Even a basic understanding of each astrology sign will help you become a better numerologist. Here's a basic overview of each of the astrology signs to get you started.

Astrology Sign Personality Traits

- **Aries (March 21–April 20)**
  Headstrong, pioneering, dynamic, courageous, impatient, impulsive, short-tempered
- **Taurus (April 21–May 21)**
  Patient, reliable, persistent, grounded, practical, stubborn, resentful, inflexible
- **Gemini (May 22–June 21)**
  Youthful, adventurous, quick-witted, communicative, inconsistent, superficial, scattered
- **Cancer (June 22–July 23)**
  Intuitive, loving, feminine, sympathetic, sensitive, insecure, possessive, moody
- **Leo (July 24–August 23)**
  Intelligent, courageous, honest, generous, short-tempered, egotistical, intolerant
- **Virgo (August 24–September 23)**
  Reliable, practical, meticulous, intelligent, analytical, worry-prone, critical, fastidious

- **Libra (September 24–October 23)**
  Idealistic, diplomatic, charming, optimistic, indecisive, changeable, extravagant
- **Scorpio (October 24–November 22)**
  Mysterious, intuitive, intense, passionate, envious, deceptive, unforgiving
- **Sagittarius (November 23–December 21)**
  Intelligent, optimistic, adventurous, honest, short-tempered, tactless, superficial
- **Capricorn (December 22–January 20)**
  Hardworking, disciplined, responsible, ambitious, materialistic, pessimistic, cynical
- **Aquarius (January 21–February 19)**
  Determined, charismatic, inventive, compassionate, rigid, contrary, unpredictable
- **Pisces (February 20–March 20)**
  Imaginative, artistic, intuitive, dreamy, selfless, indecisive, impressionable, vague

You may also wish to explore Chinese astrology, as well as the ancient Chinese principles of balance and health, for additional information. Jean Haner's book *Your Hidden Symmetry* is the perfect place to start, as is *The New Chinese Astrology* by Suzanne White.

✳

Now, let's get the ball rolling and begin with the Life Path Number.

LIFE PATH NUMBER

Your Life Path Number is the most significant number in your numerology chart. Also known as the *Ruling Number, Birth Number, Birth Path,* or *Birth Force Number,* it's the very first number a numerologist will look at to get an understanding of who you are and the kind of life you'll live. Chaldean numerology refers to it as the *Destiny Number,* because it reveals what you were born to do. In Western numerology, your Life Path Number reveals the path you've chosen to walk in this life and the lessons you've chosen to master on your journey. This number indicates the kind of life experiences you'll encounter as you fulfill your destiny and life purpose.

How to Calculate the Life Path Number

The Life Path Number is calculated from the date of birth.

The Life Path Number can be calculated by reducing down, adding across, or adding down the numbers in your date of birth; however, most numerologists consider the reducing-down and adding-across methods to be the most accurate. However, between these two methods, neither one is "better" than the other—just different. So it's simply a matter of personal preference which method you use. The rule of thumb for all three methods is to reduce a double-digit number total to a single-digit number unless it totals 11, 22, or 33. This is because 11, 22, and 33 are *Master Numbers* and do not get reduced down. We'll discuss Master Numbers a little later on.

Let's take a look at the first method: reducing down.

Method 1: Reducing Down

Step 1: Reduce the month, day, and year numbers of your birth date down to three single-digit numbers unless they total 11 or 22.

Please Note: *Some numerologists will reduce 11 and 22 down to 2 and 4 at this stage of the calculation, while some won't because they believe that 11 and 22, as Master Numbers,* *should never be reduced down regardless of where they appear. It's up to you what you prefer to do. I'm going to leave the 11 as an 11 in the example below.*

Let's use the birth date December 11, 1969 (12-11-1969), as an example:

$$\underline{1+2} \,/\, \underline{11} \,/\, \underline{1+9+6+9} = 25$$
$$\quad\textbf{3}\quad\ \ \textbf{11}\qquad\qquad\ \ \underline{2+5}$$
$$\qquad\qquad\qquad\qquad\qquad\textbf{7}$$

Step 2: Add the single totals together (and 11 and 22, where applicable, if you choose not to reduce them down) and continue to reduce down until you get a single-digit Life Path Number. If a Life Path Number totals 11, 22, or 33, it doesn't reduce down to 2, 4, or 6. It remains 11, 22, or 33 and becomes an 11/2, 22/4, or 33/6 Life Path Number.

$$\underline{3+11+7} = 21$$
$$\underline{2+1} = \textbf{3 Life Path Number}$$

Now, let's see what happens when we end up with a Master Number total for the birth date February 2, 1960 (2-2-1960):

$$\underline{2} \,/\, \underline{2} \,/\, \underline{1+9+6+0} = 16$$
$$\textbf{2}\quad\textbf{2}\qquad\qquad\ \ \underline{1+6}$$
$$\qquad\qquad\qquad\qquad\textbf{7}$$
$$\underline{2+2+7} = \textbf{11/2 Life Path Number}$$

Because 11 does not get reduced down, it remains an 11/2 Life Path Number.

✦

Some numerologists consider the reducing-down method to be the most accurate in determining a Master Number.

Let's take a look at the second and easiest method of all: adding across.

Method 2: Adding Across

Step 1: Put a plus sign between each of the individual numbers in your birth date and add across. Make sure you write the full birth year—that is, 1969 rather than just 69.

Let's use the birth date December 11, 1969 (12-11-1969), once again as an example:

1+2+1+1+1+9+6+9 = 30

Step 2: Add any double-digit numbers together until you get a single-digit Life Path Number, unless they total 11, 22, or 33, which then becomes an 11/2, 22/4, or 33/6 Life Path Number.

3+0 = **3 Life Path Number**

As you can see with our second example birth date, March 29, 1969 (3-29-1969), an extra reducing-down step is required to get a single-digit Life Path Number.

3+2+9+1+9+6+9 = 39
3+9 = 12
1+2 = **3 Life Path Number**

In some cases, you may end up with a single-digit Life Path Number in the first calculation, as in the birth date February 4, 2001 (2-4-2001):

2+4+2+0+0+1 = **9 Life Path Number**

The advantage of using the adding-across method is that the double-digit number total (compound number) prior to reducing down provides additional insights into the type of Life Path Number it is. For example, a 13/4 Life Path Number is different from a 40/4 Life Path Number because it's composed of a 1 and 3, rather than a 4 and 0. Even though both are 4 Life Path Numbers, due to the different compound-number combinations, they express themselves in slightly different ways. It pays to explore your compound numbers to gain a deeper insight into your numbers.

You will also need to take note of the 0 in compound number totals such as 10, 20, 30, 40, and so forth, prior to reducing down, as 0 amplifies the energy of the number preceding it. Chaldean numerology places the greatest emphasis on the compound number, and rightfully so.

Now let's see what happens when we use the adding-across method for the birth date February 2, 1960 (2-2-1960), which gave us a Master 11/2 Life Path Number using the reducing-down method:

$$2+2+1+9+6+0 = 20$$
$$2+0 = \textbf{2 Life Path Number}$$

As you can see, when it comes to Master Numbers, there are times when one calculation method will reveal a Master Number and another won't. Before I discuss this in further detail, let's take a look at the third and least commonly used method to calculate the Life Path Number: adding down.

Method 3: Adding Down

Step 1: Add the day, month, and year in a column.

Let's use December 11, 1969 (12-11-1969), as an example once again:

```
      12
  +   11
   1969
   1992
```

Please Note: *Another variation of this method is to reduce the year of birth down to its double-digit compound number— for example, 1969 becomes 25 (1 + 9 + 6 + 9 = 25). I'm going to leave 1969 as it is in this example.*

Step 2: Add the digits in the total across, and reduce down to a single-digit Life Path Number unless they total 11, 22, or 33, which then becomes an 11/2, 22/4, or 33/6 Life Path Number.

1+9+9+2 = 21
2+1 = **3 Life Path Number**

Now let's see what happens with the February 2, 1960 (2-2-1960), birth date that resulted in a Master 11/2 Life Path Number by reducing down and a 2 Life Path Number when adding across:

```
       2
  +    2
    1960
    1964
```
1+9+6+4 = 20

2+0 = **2 Life Path Number**

As you can see, the adding-across and adding-down methods produced a 2 Life Path Number, while the reducing-down method produced an 11/2 Life Path Number. So how do you know which method is correct? Well, that's the million-dollar question! As always, neither method is correct or incorrect—they're just different. So it's going to come down to personal preference. I don't mean to leave you hanging, but this is one of the many confusing areas in numerology where there isn't a definite one-size-fits-all answer.

Thankfully, the only time the Life Path Number calculation method becomes an issue is when you're calculating a Master Number. Because this could occur anytime you end up with a 2, 4, or 6 Life Path Number, some numerologists use all three methods and go with the majority-rule answer to determine a Master Number. Others simply choose their preferred method of calculation and stick to that. I suggest you read the Life Path Number descriptions for both 11/2 and 2, 22/4 and 4, and 33/6 and 6 in the next chapter to determine which number is the most accurate fit.

✳

Now let's take a look at the Destiny Number.

Destiny Number

In Western numerology, the *Destiny Number* is the second-most-significant number in your numerology chart and is otherwise known as the *Expression Number, Name Number,* or *Complete Name Number.* In Chaldean numerology, this number is referred to as the *Purpose Number.* Both Western and Chaldean numerologists believe that this number reveals your mission in this life and what you're destined to accomplish.

Your Destiny Number tells you what you'll be most successful doing and reveals one of the several areas of your life that must be developed in order for you to reach your full potential. Combined with the Life Path Number, this is the number to take into consideration when making career choices. Some numerologists believe that your Destiny Number is also the accumulation of your past-life achievements.

Most numerologists believe that your original birth-certificate name—whether you like it or not, and whether you currently use it or not—reveals the prechosen destiny you were born to fulfill. Even if you only had that original birth-certificate name for a short period of time and have since gone by another name as a result of marriage, adoption, or legal name change, they believe the energy from your original birth-certificate name will remain with you for life.

If you were adopted and only had your birth-certificate name for a day, that's the name that must be used to calculate your Destiny Number. Even if your original birth-certificate name was "Baby" and you only had it for two hours, you must use it. If you don't know your original birth-certificate name, you *can* calculate your adopted name instead, provided you understand that a piece of vital information is missing from your reading.

Western numerologists believe that when you change your name or use a shortened version of your birth-certificate name, your new name number doesn't erase or replace your original Destiny Number energy—it simply works alongside it, adding an extra dimension to your life, offering additional talents, abilities, opportunities, lessons, and experiences.

How to Calculate the Destiny Number

The Destiny Number is calculated from the full, original birth-certificate name.

1	2	3	4	5	6	7	8	9
A	B	C	D	E	F	G	H	I
J	K	L	M	N	O	P	Q	R
S	T	U	V	W	X	Y	Z	

Miriam Roberts

Reducing-Down Method

Step 1: Using the Western Pythagorean letters-and-numbers chart on the preceding page, write your full, original birth-certificate name and match the corresponding numbers to each letter. It pays to double-check the spelling on your birth certificate to ensure that everything is correct. You'd be surprised by how many people forget to include their middle name or have unknowingly spelled their birth-certificate name incorrectly for the majority of their lives. I believed that my middle name, Tracey, was spelled "Tracy" until I dug out my birth certificate when applying for a passport in my late teens.

Please note that a hyphenated or compound last name is considered one name, and titles such as Junior (Jr.) and Senior (Sr.) are not included in the calculation. If you don't have a middle name, you only need to calculate your first and last name. If you have several middle names, you need to calculate each middle name separately. Be sure to leave plenty of space between each letter so you don't leave out a number by mistake. Let's use the name Mary Ann Smith as an example:

M A R Y   A N N   S M I T H
4+1+9+7 1+5+5 1+4+9+2+8

Step 2: Add each name separately to create individual totals.

M A R Y   A N N   S M I T H
4+1+9+7 1+5+5 1+4+9+2+8
  21   11   24

Step 3: Add double-digit totals together to create single-number totals.

Please note: *Whether you reduce numbers 11, 22, and 33 down to 2, 4, and 6 at this stage of the calculation is another conflicting point among numerologists. Some will keep them as*

13

11, 22, and 33, because they believe a Master Number should never be reduced regardless of where it appears, and others will reduce them down. You'll have to go with your gut on this one and do whatever feels right for you. However, as you'll see in the following two examples, there are times where each method will reveal a different Destiny Number.

Let's see what happens when we reduce the 11 for Ann to a 2.

M A R Y   A N N   S M I T H
4+1+9+7 1+5+5 1+4+9+2+8
   21   11   24

2+1   1+1   2+4
3   **2**   **6**

Step 4: Add all single numbers together. Reduce them down to get a single-digit Destiny Number, unless they total 11, 22, or 33, which then becomes an 11/2, 22/4, or 33/6 Destiny Number.

3+2+6 = **11/2 Destiny Number**

Now let's see what happens when we *don't* reduce the 11 for Ann and keep it as an 11.

M A R Y   A N N   S M I T H
4+1+9+7 1+5+5 1+4+9+2+8
   21   11   24

2+1   11   2+4
3   11   6

3+11+6 = 20
2+0 = **2 Destiny Number**

Please note: *Another version of the reducing-down method's step 3 is to add the double-digit compound numbers* *together rather than reduce to single-digit numbers. For example, 21 + 11 + 24 = 56. Since 5 + 6 = 11, this would result in an 11/2 Destiny Number.*

As you can see, when it comes to Master Numbers, there are times when the calculation methods reveal different answers. Before I discuss this in further detail, let's take a look at the adding-across method.

Adding-Across Method

Another way to calculate a Destiny Number is to simply add the numbers across, and reduce any double-digit numbers down to get a single-digit Destiny Number—unless they total 11, 22, or 33, which then becomes an 11/2, 22/4, or 33/6 Destiny Number.

MARY   ANN   SMITH
4+1+9+7 + 1+5+5 + 1+4+9+2+8 = 56

5+6 = 11/2 Destiny Number

So how do you know if Mary's Destiny Number is a Master Number 11/2 or a 2? That's another million-dollar question!

As with the Life Path Number calculation method, it's simply a matter of personal choice, because there isn't a definite answer. Thankfully, the only time the name-calculation method becomes an issue is when you're calculating a Master Number. I suggest you read the number descriptions for both the 11/2 and 2, 22/4 and 4, or 33/6 and 6 Destiny Numbers in the next chapter to determine which is the most accurate fit. Another option is to go with the majority-rule answer.

Before we move on to the Soul Number, bear in mind that you'll be using the same letters-and-numbers chart and your preferred calculation method to work out your Current Name Number later in this chapter, as well as a Business Name Number, Pet Name Number, and Street Name Number in Part III. So you might want to bookmark this section.

Soul Number

In Western numerology, the *Soul Number*—otherwise known as the *Soul's Urge, Soul Desire,* or *Heart's Desire Number*—is the next significant number in your numerology chart. Your Soul Number reveals what motivates you and what you need in order to feed your soul. In other words, it reveals what your heart desires and what your soul urges you to accomplish in this life in order to feel content.

(Sometimes the hustle and bustle of everyday life can quiet the calling of your soul, and it can be difficult to determine what your soul is longing for. This is why practices such as meditation, yoga, conscious breathing, qigong, and quiet alone time are so important. They allow your soul to communicate its needs via your intuition. Even when you're unable to practice these activities, your soul is constantly making its needs known to you—all you have to do is listen.)

How to Calculate the Soul Number

The Soul Number is calculated from the vowels in the birth-certificate name.

> **Please note:** *In Chaldean numerology, the letter Y is always considered a vowel; however, in Western numerology, Y is sometimes a consonant, and other times it's a vowel. Most Western numerologists consider Y a vowel when there are no other vowels in the syllable or when the Y is next to (or in between) two consonants, such as in the names Wynn, Yvette, and Lucy. Some numerologists also consider Y a vowel when*

it is preceded by another vowel in a syllable and together they provide the vowel sound, such as in the names Tracey, Kaylene, and Boyle. And if that isn't confusing enough, other numerologists consider W a vowel when it is preceded by another vowel in a syllable and together they provide the vowel sound or when it appears between two vowels. However, due to conflicting theories among numerologists, there are even variations within these rules. Once again, you're going to have to go with whatever feels best for you.

Reducing-Down Method

Step 1: Add up the numbers in your birth-certificate name that are vowels.

Step 2: Add each name separately to create individual totals. Add double-digit totals together to create single-number totals.

```
M A R Y   A N N   S M I T H
  1 7 1   1         9
  1 + 7   1         9
    8
```

Please note: *As with the Destiny Number, whether you reduce numbers 11, 22, or 33 down to 2, 4, or 6 at this stage of the calculation is your personal choice. As previously mentioned, some numerologists will keep them as 11, 22, and 33 because they believe a Master Number should never be reduced regardless of where it appears.*

Step 3: Add all single numbers together. Reduce them down to get a single-digit Soul Number, unless they total 11, 22, or 33, which then becomes an 11/2, 22/4, or 33/6 Soul Number.

8+1+9 = 18
1+8 = **9 Soul Number**

Please note: *Another version of the reducing-down method's step 2 is to add any double-digit compound numbers together rather than reduce to single-digit numbers.*

Adding-Across Method

Add the numbers across, and reduce any double-digit numbers down to get a single-digit Soul Number, unless they total 11, 22, or 33, which then becomes an 11/2, 22/4, or 33/6 Soul Number. As you can see in this particular example, the adding-across method reveals the same answer.

M A R Y   A N N   S M I T H
  1 7 1   9

1+7+1+9 = 18
1+8 = **9 Soul Number**

Now, let's take a look at the Personality Number.

PERSONALITY NUMBER

Even though the *Personality Number* is one of the 7 Core Numbers in your chart, its influence is less dominant than the Life Path, Destiny, and Soul Numbers. Your Personality Number is said to represent the "outer you," or the side of yourself you're willing to show others (rather than its being a reflection of your true inner nature), which is why it's otherwise known as the *Outer You* or *Outer Personality Number.*

Because you're in charge of the image you project to others, the Personality Number doesn't always reflect your true nature.

Instead, it reflects the censored impression you choose to give off and the way in which you're perceived by others. It isn't uncommon for the stronger personality traits of the astrology sign, Life Path, Destiny, Soul, and Birth Day Numbers to overshadow the Personality Number traits, so it's perfectly normal if you don't identify with your Personality Number.

How to Calculate the Personality Number

The Personality Number is calculated from the consonants in the birth-certificate name.

Reducing-Down Method

Step 1: Add the numbers in your birth-certificate name that are consonants.

Step 2: Add each name separately to create individual totals. Add double-digit totals together to create single-number totals.

M A R Y	A N N	S M I T H
4 + 9	5+5	1+4 +2+8
13	10	15
1+3	1+0	1+5
4	**1**	**6**

Please note: *As with the Destiny and Soul Numbers, whether you reduce numbers 11, 22, or 33 down to 2, 4, or 6 at this stage of the calculation is your personal choice. As previously mentioned, some numerologists will keep them as 11, 22, and 33 because they believe a Master Number should never be reduced regardless of where it appears.*

Step 3: Add all single numbers together. Reduce them down to get a single-digit Personality Number, unless they total 11, 22, or 33, which then becomes an 11/2, 22/4, or 33/6 Personality Number.

4+1+6 = **11/2 Personality Number**

Please note: *Another version of the reducing-down method's step 2 is to add any double-digit compound numbers together rather than reduce to single-digit numbers. For example, 13 + 10 + 15 = 38. Since 3 + 8 = 11, this would result in an 11/2 Personality Number.*

Adding-Across Method

Add the numbers across, and reduce any double-digit numbers down to a single-digit Personality Number, unless they total 11, 22, or 33, which then becomes an 11/2, 22/4, or 33/6 Personality Number. As you can see in this example, the adding-across method reveals the same answer.

```
M A R Y   A N N   S M I T H
4 + 9     5+5    1+4 +2+8
```

4+9+5+5+1+4+2+8 = 38
3+8 = **11/2 Personality Number**

✳

Now let's take a look at the Maturity Number.

MATURITY NUMBER

The *Maturity Number* is a very important number in your chart because it reveals your future potential and the ultimate goal of your life. It's also known as the *Power Number, Attainment Number, Realization Number,* or *True Self* because it pinpoints your position of personal power and where your destiny is leading you. If you want to know what your life is preparing you for and what to expect from the second half of your life, your Maturity Number will tell you. Chaldean numerology refers to this number as the *Life Goal.*

Interestingly, your Maturity Number doesn't kick in until "maturity" or midlife, when you have gained a better understanding of yourself and your path. Some numerologists believe that this isn't until you reach your fourth Challenge and Pinnacle (discussed in Part II); however, this is disputable. Since we mature at differing rates, the Maturity Number commencement age can vary from person to person, but it generally kicks off between 35 and 45 and is fully functional by the age of 50.

As each year passes, the energy of your Maturity Number strengthens and matures. In other words, the older you get, the stronger the influence your Maturity Number has upon your personality and your life. It pays to keep this number in mind when making long-term goals and decisions.

How to Calculate the Maturity Number

The Maturity Number is calculated by adding the Life Path Number and Destiny Number together. Or, in Chaldean numerology, the Life Goal Number is calculated by adding the Destiny Number and Purpose Number together.

Step 1: Add your Life Path Number and Destiny Number together.

Please note: *Some numerologists will reduce an 11/2, 22/4, or 33/6 Life Path or Destiny Number down to 2, 4, or 6 at this stage of the calculation, while some won't because they*

21

believe a Master Number should never be reduced regardless of where it appears. It's your personal choice what you prefer to do.

Step 2: Add any double-digit totals together to create a single-digit Maturity Number unless they total 11, 22, or 33, which then becomes an 11/2, 22/4, or 33/6 Maturity Number.

Let's use Mary Ann Smith's 3 Life Path Number and 11/2 Destiny Number as an example.

> 3 Life Path Number + 11/2 Destiny Number = 14
> 1+4 = **5 Maturity Number**

✳

Now let's move on to your Birth Day Number.

Birth Day Number

The *Birth Day Number,* otherwise known as the *Day Number* or *Day Born Number,* is another important aspect of your numerology profile because it indicates special talents and abilities that will assist you on your life path toward fulfilling your destiny. Some numerologists believe that the Birth Day Number has the greatest influence over the middle years of your life, while others believe it reveals your personality strengths and challenges. Either way, your Birth Day Number is the easiest number to work out because it's simply the "day" number of your birth date.

How to Calculate the Birth Day Number

The Birth Day Number is the day of the month of a birth date.

Reduce the day of your birth date to a single-digit number. If you were born on a single-digit day, that is your Birth Day Number, and if you were born on a double-digit day, add the numbers to-gether to get a single-digit Birth Day Number. If you were born on the 11th or 29th, it would become an 11/2 or 29/11/2 Birth Day Number, and a birthday on the 22nd is a 22/4 Birth Day Number. For example:

> May 9, 1972 = **9 Birth Day Number**
> June 24, 1983 = <u>2+4</u> = **6 Birth Day Number**
> October 29, 2001 = <u>2+9</u> = **29/11/2 Birth Day Number** (refer to the description for the 11/2 Birth Day Number)
> February 22, 1954 = **22/4 Birth Day Number**

Please note: *As with the Life Path Number, it pays to bear in mind the original double-digit compound number prior to reducing down to a single number, as it provides additional insight into the type of Birth Day Number it is. For example, a 23/5 Birth Day Number is different from a 14/5 Birth Day Number because it's composed of a 2 and 3 rather than a 1 and 4. Even though both are 5 Birth Day Numbers, due to the differ-ent compound-number combinations, they express themselves in slightly different ways. By exploring your compound num-bers, you will gain a deeper insight into your numbers. You will also need to take note of the 0 in compound Birth Day Numbers such as 10, 20, and 30 prior to reducing down, as 0 amplifies the energy of the number preceding it.*

✳

Now let's take a look at the final name number in a numerolo-gy chart: the Current Name Number.

CURRENT NAME NUMBER

In Western numerology, the *Current Name Number,* otherwise known as the *Minor Expression Number,* is the current first and last name you use on a daily basis. This is the name you would have on your business card or the name you would use to sign a petition. It may be a shortened version of your original birth-certificate name or a new name altogether due to marriage, adoption, or some other reason. Either way, your Current Name Number is the first and last name you go by today.

As previously mentioned, Western numerologists believe that the Destiny Number calculated from your original birth-certificate name reveals the destiny and life mission you've chosen to fulfill in this lifetime; therefore, its governing influence cannot be erased by changing your name or by using a shortened version of your original birth-certificate name. With that being said, your Current Name Number still has a major influence on your life because it offers additional traits, strengths, lessons, experiences, and opportunities to assist you on your journey. In other words, your Current Name Number works *alongside* your existing Destiny Number, rather than replaces it.

How to Calculate the Current Name Number

The Current Name Number is calculated from the first and last name used on a daily basis.

The same method is used to calculate your Current Name Number as is used to calculate your Destiny Number. Remember, a hyphenated or compound last name is considered one name, and titles such as Junior (Jr.) or Senior (Sr.) are not included in the calculation. Be sure to leave plenty of space between each letter so you don't leave out a number by mistake.

Feel free to use the reducing-down or adding-across method, or both, to calculate your Current Name Number. Let's use Mary Ann Smith's current and married name, Mary Jones, as an example:

Reducing-Down Method

M A R Y   J O N E S
4+1+9+7 1+6+5+5+1
   21   18
   2+1 = 3   1+8 = 9

3+9 = 12
1+2 = **3 Current Name Number**

Adding-Across Method

M A R Y   J O N E S
4+1+9+7 +1+6+5+5+1 = **39**

3+9 = 12
1+2 = **3 Current Name Number**

✳

Now that you've calculated the 7 Core Numbers from your date of birth, original birth-certificate name, and current first and last name, let's take a look at the Karmic Lesson Numbers—another significant aspect of your numerology profile.

KARMIC LESSON NUMBERS

One of the reasons why you've chosen to incarnate into this current life is to learn to master some of your inherited weaknesses from previous lives. Your *Karmic Lesson Numbers* indicate what those weaknesses are, along with the specific areas in need of growth that must be addressed in this life. Some numerologists believe that a Karmic Lesson Number indicates a number, or energy, you haven't experienced in previous lives and therefore need to develop in *this* life. One thing's for certain: if you have a Karmic Lesson Number in your numerology chart, that karmic lesson will continually present itself throughout your life until you master it once and for all.

The average number of Karmic Lesson Numbers in a chart is 2; however, some people have more than 2, and others have none. Still, if you're fortunate enough not to have any Karmic Lesson Numbers, it doesn't mean you're going to have an easy, trouble-free life. It simply means that the majority of your challenges will come through the other numbers in your chart. Believe me, I have no Karmic Lesson Numbers in my chart, and my life has been far from easy and lesson-free.

Here's some good news for those who *do* have Karmic Lesson Numbers: the influence of the karmic lesson is greatly minimized when that number is one of your Core Numbers, such as your Life Path, Destiny, Soul, Personality, Maturity, or Birth Day Number. For example, if you have a Karmic Lesson Number 7 and you're a 7 Life Path, the karmic lesson is reduced. On the other hand, if you have the same Challenge Number (defined in Part II) as your Karmic Lesson Number, it emphasizes the lesson. Sorry to cheer you up and then rain on your parade!

So, let's start working out your Karmic Lesson Numbers by referring back to your Western numerology Destiny Number calculations based on your original birth-certificate name.

How to Calculate the Karmic Lesson Numbers

Karmic Lesson Numbers are calculated from the missing numbers between 1 and 9 in a birth-certificate name, indicating karmic lessons.

If every number between 1 and 9 is present, then you have no karmic lessons; however, any number that is missing is a Karmic Lesson Number. Let's take a look at Mary Ann Smith's name to see if she has any Karmic Lesson Numbers.

MARY   ANN   SMITH
4197   155   14928

As you can see, Mary is missing numbers 3 and 6 from her name; therefore, she has a 3 Karmic Lesson Number and a 6 Karmic Lesson Number.

Because Mary has a 3 Life Path Number and 3 Current Name Number, the influence of her 3 Karmic Lesson Number is minimized (*whew*, lucky break, Mary!). However, because she doesn't have a number 6 among her Core Numbers, she'll need to overcome her 6 Karmic Lesson Number in this lifetime.

✳

Congratulations on making it this far! Pat yourself on the back for calculating your 7 Core Numbers and your Karmic Lesson Numbers, too. Before we move on to the number meanings, let's recap your numbers and what each chart position means:

7 Core Numbers	
Your Life Path Number is: _____	The path you will walk in this life
Your Destiny Number is: _____	What you're destined to become
Your Soul Number is: _____	What your soul needs in order to feel content
Your Personality Number is: _____	How others perceive you
Your Maturity Number is: _____	Your future potential from age 35 to 45 and onward
Your Birth Day Number is: _____	Your natural talents and abilities
Your Current Name Number is: _____	Your additional strengths, lessons, and experiences

Karmic Lesson Numbers	
Your Karmic Lesson Numbers are: _____	Your weaknesses and areas in need of growth

Although it isn't one of your 7 Core Numbers, it pays to be mindful of your *First Name Number* (the total of your first name), because this number uncovers further personality traits and tendencies to assist you on your path. Another number of less significance that can affect the way you see the world is the *Cornerstone Number,* which is the first letter of your first name. This number reveals your attitude toward life and how you perceive the world around you. Some numerologists believe that the first vowel of your first name uncovers your deeper, hidden self, whereas others believe that it reveals your spiritual and philosophical approach to life. Most numerologists agree, however, that your *Last Name Number* (the total of your last name) represents the inherited ancestral traits of the family.

✦ ✦ ✦

Number Meanings

Now let's take a look at the meanings of the numbers that apply to both Western and Chaldean numerology (and other numerology systems, too).

NUMBER 1: THE INDEPENDENT INDIVIDUAL

Number 1s are the Independent Individuals and leaders of the world, and their greatest gift is their uniqueness and originality. They're strong-minded, self-sufficient, and extremely capable; however, they often feel like an outsider or a square peg in a round hole. On the one hand, they want to belong and be a part of the team—yet on the other, they crave to be #1 so they can stand out from the crowd. Once they learn to lead *alongside* others rather than dominating from above, they make outstanding managers and leaders.

Number 1s rarely accept defeat, and they never, ever give up. When they feel mentally stimulated and challenged, they can build highly successful careers. With a knack for inventing creative yet practical solutions to everyday challenges and dilemmas,

1s are talented problem solvers who think outside the box. Even though they prefer to start things rather than finish them, they like to take the bull by the horns and try their best to get things done. If a 1 lacks the confidence and motivation to be independent, lead, or take control, he or she must learn to adopt those traits throughout the course of this life in order to balance the energy of his or her 1.

Life is a journey of self-discovery for all of us, but for 1s, that's their life purpose. Self-awareness, along with an understanding of how they relate to others, is their main area in need of focus in this life. When living in the positive, 1s are gifted and innovative thinkers with extremely creative minds. By using creative visualization to direct their powerful thoughts toward the accomplishment of their goals, they can manifest their dreams with greater ease. Once they've worked through their self-confidence and identity issues, they have much potential for success. Groundbreaking pioneers, 1s pave the way toward new-and-improved ways of life. Despite their abrupt tone, intolerance, and hypersensitivity to criticism, they're the people we turn to for leadership and guidance.

1's Strengths

- Independent
- Pioneering
- Courageous
- Innovative
- Original
- Self-motivated
- Determined
- Strong-willed
- Creative
- Trendsetting

1's *Weaknesses*

- Impatient
- Insecure
- Egotistical
- Self-centered
- Controlling
- Competitive
- Abrupt
- Bossy
- Opinionated
- Aggressive

Life Lessons

The major lessons number 1s need to learn in this lifetime are:

- To become self-aware
- To harmonize with others
- To embrace their individuality
- To utilize their creative power
- To be diplomatic, patient, and tolerant
- To lead alongside others
- To love and believe in themselves
- To master their aggression

Astrological Equivalent

Most astrologers believe the astrological equivalent to number 1 is Leo; however, some feel it also resonates with Aries and Aquarius.

Suitable Career Choices

Independent contractor; business owner; manager; team leader; entrepreneur; inventor; consultant; sales, marketing, or advertising professional; print or broadcast journalist; writer; life coach; designer; engineer; musician; actor; entertainer; public speaker; politician; real-estate broker; executive, media professional; financial advisor; creative director.

Compatibility

1s are said to be most compatible with numbers 3, 4, 5, 7, and 22/4.

1 Life Path Number

As a 1 Life Path, you're here to walk the path of the Independent Individual so you can break away from the pack and dance to a different tune. There will be times when you'll feel different and possibly alienated and alone; however, you must use your uniqueness to your advantage rather than allow it to cause you to feel separated from the whole. Your individuality is your gift to the world, and the sooner you believe this, the sooner you'll improve your quality of life.

As a 1 Life Path, life will force you to step up to the plate and stand on your own two feet, so you must find the strength and courage to dare to believe in yourself. Don't let your competitive nature get the better of you, because there's no such thing as competition in the Universe. When you truly know and believe that we're all connected, you can begin to reach your full potential. As a 1 Life Path, you're fulfilling your life purpose when you lovingly lead others toward something that contributes to the greater good.

1 Destiny Number

As a 1 Destiny, you're destined to be an Independent Individual who embraces your uniqueness and uses it to your advantage. Your life mission is to walk the path less traveled and assist those in need of leadership and guidance. You may run your own business, work autonomously, or be a manager of others. Either way, you're destined to have the courage to think for yourself. You are fully empowered when you focus on your strengths rather than your fears. You're a creative and innovative self-starter, so put your talents to good use.

1 Soul Number

As a 1 Soul, you long to become an Independent Individual who embraces your uniqueness and thinks outside the box. In your heart of hearts, all your soul wants is for you to have the freedom to be yourself and not repress who you are in order to fit in. As a 1 Soul, you're motivated by being in charge and initiating projects. You don't like being told what to do, and you're not meant to follow the crowd. When you have the courage to believe in yourself and step out on your own, you'll fulfill your heart's desire.

1 Personality Number

As a 1 Personality, you may be perceived as being opinionated, courageous, and strong. Others may see you as the person in charge who takes control of a situation and sorts everything out. Due to your unique style and mode of expression, you may come

33

across as a trendsetter or someone who stands out from the crowd. Even those who perceive you as intimidating and bossy will often trust your judgment and turn to you for guidance.

1 Maturity Number

With a 1 Maturity Number, life is steering you toward becoming an Independent Individual who embraces your individuality and uses it to your advantage. Your life's goal is to become a kind and compassionate leader who sets the stage for new-and-improved ways of thinking, living, and being. As you mature, you'll find yourself becoming more independent, confident, and self-aware. A 1 Maturity Number also indicates having the courage, willpower, and determination to achieve your goals.

1 Birth Day Number (1st, 10th, 19th, and 28th)

As a 1 Birth Day, you're gifted with the ability to lead and take control. Your motivation, determination, and drive enable you to reach your goals; however, your impatience and intolerance can cause you much distress. You enjoy asserting your individuality and expressing your creativity, and your dislike of being told what to do can cause friction with authority figures. You're humorous and charismatic and have a strong personality.

1 Current Name Number

A 1 Current Name enhances your independence, individuality, creativity, and strength. It also enables you to lead and take control of your life. This number will help you work autonomously, run your own business, manage others, and stand on your own two feet. This is the number of the groundbreaking pioneer who likes to be #1.

1 Karmic Lesson Number

Throughout the course of this life, you'll need to adopt the characteristics of number 1 by being more independent, courageous, and motivated. There will be times when you'll need to stand up for yourself and your beliefs regardless of the outcome and despite others' opinions. This karmic lesson will force you to embrace your individuality and walk the path less traveled with your head held high.

1 Checklist*

To determine whether you're fully embracing your "1-ness," ask yourself these questions:

- *Am I walking the path less traveled, leading others, or being a leader in my field?*

- *Am I asserting my independence and standing on my own two feet?*

- *Am I using my creative mind and innovative ideas to manifest my dreams?*

- *Am I looking at new-and-improved ways of doing things?*

1 Example

Civil rights activist and Nobel Peace Prize winner Martin Luther King, Jr. (1/15/1929), is a classic example of a 1 Life Path living his life purpose as an Independent Individual and leader. The strength, courge, and determination of his number 1 enabled him to become a groundbreaking pioneer for racial equality for African Americans during the 1950s and '60s. Martin Luther King dreamed of a nation where people were judged by the content of their character, rather than the color of their skin—and thanks

---

*Checklist applies to everyone with a 1 among their Core Numbers.

to him, massive changes have been made throughout the world. Thank you, Martin Luther King, Jr., for your vision of a better world and for having the courage to take a stand. Thank you for reminding humanity that we're all equal despite our physical and personal differences!

1 Affirmation

"I embrace my strength, individuality, and independence."

NUMBER 2: THE COOPERATIVE PEACEMAKER

Number 2s are the Cooperative Peacemakers of the world, and their greatest gift is their extraordinary ability to heal people and the environment around them. They're natural mediators who have a talent for smoothing things over, and their knack for seeing both sides of a situation enables them to arrive at a harmonious outcome for all. Number 2s have big hearts and an enormous capacity to love. They thrive on connection and companionship and will do anything in their power to ensure that everyone feels happy and loved.

Due to a fear of confrontation and overwhelming desire to please, 2s have trouble saying no, which often causes them to be doormats for others. Rather than be honest about their feelings and risk upsetting those around them in the process, they tend to become martyrs, hiding their unhappiness or resentment behind their smiles. (This isn't such an issue when they have a self-assured astrology profile or strong, dominant Core Numbers such as 1, 4, 6, 8, and 9 in their chart.) They prefer being part of a twosome rather than being on their own, and because they're sensitive to negative energy, they require a healthy, harmonious environment at all times. Regular exercise and meditation, a healthy diet, and loving friendships and partnerships are vital to their well-being. Many are musically gifted or are passionate lovers of music.

Number 2s are great support people who prefer to work on the finer details behind the scenes. They're wonderful listeners and have an intuitive sense of timing, especially when it comes to other people and their needs. They must learn to attain balance in every area of their lives, whether it's finding the balance between giving and receiving or between their home life and career, or learning how to balance their emotions. Even though their hypersensitivity and insecurity can cause them anxiety and distress, they make fantastic parents, friends, and partners and are the ultimate team members and players. Patient, gentle, and kind, 2s embody a nurturing, feminine energy that is an asset to this world.

2's Strengths

- Cooperative
- Loving
- Harmonious
- Feminine
- Nurturing
- Patient
- Creative
- Affectionate
- Intuitive
- Supportive

2's Weaknesses

- Critical
- Moody
- Hypersensitive
- Jealous

- Lazy
- Self-conscious
- Indecisive
- Codependent
- Shy
- Weak

Life Lessons

The major life lessons number 2s need to learn in this lifetime are:

- To love and believe in themselves
- To define their personal limits and boundaries
- To find the strength to say no
- To trust their intuition
- To embrace their independence
- To be honest about their feelings
- To master their sensitivity
- To attain balance and harmony

Astrological Equivalent

Most astrologers believe the astrological equivalent to number 2 is Cancer; however, some feel it also resonates with Libra.

Suitable Career Choices

Counselor, healer, nurse, veterinary technician, caregiver, stay-at-home mom or dad, chef, mediator, negotiator, politician, tailor, musician, clairvoyant, artist, writer, social worker, teacher, child-care professional, personal assistant, diplomat, administrator, alternative therapist, physical therapist, nutritionist, hairstylist, makeup artist, bookkeeper, cosmetologist, guidance counselor, psychologist, massage therapist, event planner.

Compatibility

Number 2s are said to be most compatible with numbers 2, 3, 4, 6, 9, 11/2, 22/4, and 33/6.

2 Life Path Number

As a 2 Life Path, you're here to walk the path of the Cooperative Peacemaker to promote harmony within your family, circle of friends, workplace, and community. You're a wonderful listener and a natural counselor, with an ability to heal others both energetically and verbally. You'll do anything for those you love and enjoy helping people improve their lives. You dedicate yourself to your relationships and are the first person to "kiss and make up" after an argument, but you need to learn to stand up for yourself and not allow others to take you for granted. As a 2 Life Path, you're fulfilling your life purpose when you love, nurture, support, and heal those around you, provided that you don't sacrifice your own needs in the process in order to avoid confrontations.

2 Destiny Number

As a 2 Destiny, you're destined to be a Cooperative Peacemaker who promotes peace within your family, circle of friends, workplace, and community. Your life's mission is to support and heal others, and find peaceful resolution to conflict. You may be a support person behind the scenes in your personal life or career. You might even be a mediator, healer, or counselor who enjoys helping people, animals, or the environment and being part of a team. As a 2 Destiny, you likely have creative, artistic, intuitive, teaching, or musical abilities . . . so put them to good use!

2 Soul Number

As a 2 Soul, you long to be a Cooperative Peacemaker who promotes peace and harmony within your family, circle of friends, workplace, and community. In your heart of hearts, all your soul wants is to thrive in a harmonious environment where everyone is happy. This explains why you can easily see both sides of an argument and promote a peaceful resolution. As a 2 Soul, you're motivated by love, harmony, friendship, and the relationships in your life. As you support, nurture, love, and heal others, you fulfill your heart's desire.

2 Personality Number

As a 2 Personality, you may be perceived as being a Co-operative Peacemaker who promotes harmony within your family, circle of friends, workplace, or community. You may come across as a genuine, likable, and kindhearted person who can be trusted with personal information. People will open up to you because they sense your nonjudgmental viewpoints and authentic desire to help. Even though you may be perceived as a pushover, you have a knack for helping others feel better about themselves and their problems.

2 Maturity Number

With a 2 Maturity Number, life is steering you toward becoming a Cooperative Peacemaker who promotes harmony within your family, circle of friends, workplace, and community. Your life's goal is to heal and support others and to find peaceful resolution to conflict. As you mature, you'll find yourself becoming more intuitive, sensitive, and compassionate toward others. A 2 Maturity Number also indicates harmonious relationships with others and opportunities to expand your creative and intuitive abilities.

2 Birth Day Number (2nd, 11th, 20th, and 29th)

As a 2 Birth Day, you're gifted with the ability to work harmoniously with others and to recognize their needs. You're cooperative, sensitive, and understanding, and crave meaningful connections with loved ones and friends. You're a giver rather than a taker and need to find the balance between giving and receiving. You have a good eye for detail, and you're the power behind the throne.

2 Current Name Number

A 2 Current Name enhances your intuition, sensitivity, and ability to love and heal. It also enables you to see both sides of a situation and promote a peaceful resolution to conflicts. This number will help you be a good support person, mediator, counselor, partner, and team member. This is the number of the intuitive, musician, and caregiver.

2 Karmic Lesson Number

Throughout the course of this life, you'll need to adopt the characteristics of number 2 by being more cooperative, understanding, and patient toward others. There will be times when you'll need to be more sensitive to others' emotions, opinions, and needs in order to create a harmonious environment or to work more effectively as a team. This karmic lesson will force you to be more diplomatic and considerate, and more caring to those around you.

2 Checklist

To determine whether you're fully embracing your "2-ness," ask yourself these questions:

- *Do I promote peace and harmony among the people and situations I encounter?*

- *Do I listen to my intuition and follow my inner guidance at all times?*

- *Am I kind, considerate, and supportive?*

- *Do I embrace every opportunity I'm given to nurture, support, counsel, or heal others with love?*

2 Example

Angel Therapist and best-selling author Doreen Virtue (4-29-1958) is a classic example of a 2 Life Path (using the reducing-down and adding-down methods) or Master Number 11/2 Life Path (using the adding-across method) with a Master Number 29/11/2 Birth Day whose life purpose is to be the Cooperative Peacemaker and Inspirational Teacher/Spiritual Messenger. With a doctorate in counseling psychology, Doreen is a gifted clairvoyant and speaker who is also an advocate for many charities involving the environment, animal rights, and children. Thank you, Doreen, for your contribution to humanity and planet Earth, and for teaching us about the angels!

2 Affirmation

"I nurture, love, and heal myself and others."

NUMBER 3: THE SELF-EXPRESSIVE CREATIVE

Number 3s are the artists and creators of the world, and their greatest gift is their ability to uplift and inspire. The childlike 3s are fun loving and young at heart and have a talent for working with children. They're born entertainers who can light up a room with their smiles. Despite their tendency to criticize and gossip, their charisma is contagious and draws people in like magnets. Number 3s are bubbly, bright, and witty, and have a fabulous sense of humor.

Self-expression—whether it's artistic, kinesthetic, verbal, or conceptual—is their key to happiness. When they express themselves using their hands, bodies, words, visions, and ideas, they improve their overall well-being and quality of life. There are three types of creative 3s: those who are artistically creative, those with creative concepts and ideas, and those who are creatively gifted with words. *All* 3s are destined to discover their creative gifts in this life so they can develop and express them on a regular basis. They are often drawn to the literary, visual, or performing arts.

Unless 3s have a grounding astrology chart or other, grounding Core Numbers such as 4 and 8, a lack of self-discipline and inability to focus can result in disorganized and sometimes chaotic lives, due to the scattered energy of number 3. Extra effort is usually required to finish what they start and to achieve mental, emotional, physical, and financial stability. Number 3s have the gift of the gab, but they often struggle to identify their innermost feelings and put those feelings into words. During the course of their lives, they must learn to speak their truth. Even though they can be critical and melodramatic at times, they're optimistic, outgoing, and friendly, and are seldom down for long. Once they overcome their self-doubt, they can step into their full power and actualize their dreams. Number 3s are the happy "sunshine" people who brighten up the world.

3's Strengths

- Creative
- Optimistic
- Humorous
- Friendly
- Inspirational
- Imaginative
- Fun
- Outgoing
- Charismatic
- Gifted with words

3's Weaknesses

- Critical
- Melodramatic
- Dishonest
- Disorganized
- Scattered
- Gossipy
- Irresponsible
- Superficial
- Attention seeking
- Conceited

Life Lessons

The major life lessons number 3s need to learn in this lifetime are:

- To overcome their self-doubt

- To focus, plan, and prioritize

- To express themselves creatively

- To speak their truth

- To communicate their emotions and put their feelings into words

- To attain emotional balance

- To eliminate unnecessary drama

- To minimize negative self-expression

Astrological Equivalent

Most astrologers believe the astrological equivalent to number 3 is Sagittarius; however, some feel that it also resonates with Pisces and Leo.

Suitable Career Choices

Entertainer; communications professional; artist; chef; landscaper; designer; actor; musician; dancer; comedian; child-care professional; teacher; writer; publicist; photographer; clairvoyant; healer; jewelry maker; florist; salesperson; shop assistant; color consultant; socialite; architect; bartender; waiter/waitress; graphic/web designer; hairstylist; cosmetologist; makeup artist; life coach; personal trainer; or literary, visual, or performing artist (anything creative).

Compatibility

Number 3s are said to be most compatible with numbers 1, 2, 3, 5, 6, 9, 11/2, and 33/6.

3 Life Path Number

As a 3 Life Path, you're here to walk the path of the Self-Expressive Creative so you can use your creative and communicative abilities to bring joy into the world. When you use your gift with words, your artistic talents, or your creative ideas to uplift and inspire, you're fulfilling your life purpose as a 3. Your imagination, sense of humor, and ability to entertain are the tools you've been given to help you in your quest. When you put them to good use, you'll improve your overall well-being and your quality of life. Life will encourage you, as a 3 Life Path, to speak honestly from the heart and to overcome your tendency to express yourself negatively by gossiping, exaggerating, criticizing, or complaining. Once you realize that your words are affirmations, you'll see that you're only hurting yourself.

3 Destiny Number

As a 3 Destiny, you're destined to be a Self-Expressive Creative who uses your artistic and communicative abilities to bring joy into the world. Your life's mission is to encourage, uplift, and inspire others with your imagination, sense of humor, artistic talents, and/or your flair with the spoken or written word. As a 3 Destiny, you must learn to focus, prioritize, and take action in order to achieve your goals; otherwise you may risk becoming a jack-of-all-trades and master of none. When you combine your talent and passion with your determination and drive, and follow through with practical action, you can reach your full potential and make your dreams come true. You have a gift for counseling and motivating others, so put it to good use!

3 Soul Number

As a 3 Soul, you long to express yourself and use your creative and communicative abilities to bring joy into the world. In your heart of hearts, all your soul wants is to be joyful and happy and for others to be happy, too. You feel that life is meant to be fun, so you live it to the fullest. As a 3 Soul, you're motivated by people, conversation, laughter, entertainment, and the arts. As you express yourself verbally and creatively, you fulfill your heart's desire.

3 Personality Number

As a 3 Personality, you may be perceived as being a friendly and outgoing entertainer who enjoys people, conversation, and being the center of attention. You come across as magnetic, optimistic, and charming or as a flighty social butterfly who brightens up the room. Try to be honest, authentic, and sincere—and override your tendency to gossip—in order to make the best impression.

3 Maturity Number

With a 3 Maturity Number, life is steering you toward expressing yourself and using your creative and communicative abilities to bring joy into the world. Your life's goal is use your talents to uplift and inspire others as well as yourself. As you mature, you'll find yourself becoming more extroverted, social, and charismatic, and cultivating a gift with words. A 3 Maturity Number also indicates an active social life and enhanced creative abilities.

3 Birth Day Number (3rd, 12th, 21st, and 30th)

As a 3 Birth Day, you're gifted with the ability to communicate effectively with others, and you were born to express yourself verbally and creatively. You're outgoing, optimistic, and friendly and can see the brighter side of life. You're fun loving and enthusiastic and have a great sense of humor. You have much potential for success, but you'll need to concentrate and focus if you want to achieve your goals.

3 Current Name Number

A 3 Current Name enhances your creative talents and your ability to express yourself. It also enhances your ability to speak your truth and communicate more effectively with others. This number will help you see the fun side of life, form many friendships, bring joy into the world, and uplift and inspire others— provided that you can overcome your tendency to criticize and gossip.

3 Karmic Lesson Number

Throughout the course of this life, you'll need to adopt the characteristics of number 3 by being more creative and optimistic. There will be times when you'll need to work hard to put your feelings into words rather than just criticize and complain. This karmic lesson will force you to express yourself creatively and focus on achieving your goals.

3 Checklist

To determine whether you're fully embracing your "3-ness," ask yourself these questions:

- *Do I express myself creatively, artistically, or verbally on a regular basis?*
- *Am I a bringer of joy, hope, happiness, and laughter?*
- *Do I uplift and inspire others to feel better about themselves and their lives?*

- *Am I speaking my truth and communicating my thoughts and feelings?*

3 Example

Internationally acclaimed singer/songwriter Celine Dion (3-30-1968), with her 3 Life Path and 3 Birth Day, is a classic example of a Self-Expressive Creative fulfilling her life purpose by uplifting others through music. World-renowned comedienne Joan Rivers (6-8-1933), with her 3 Life Path and 3 Soul, is another classic example, fulfilling her life purpose by using her creative abilities to express herself and uplift others through humor. Celine, your beautiful music has helped raise the vibration of the world; and Joan, your outrageous sense of humor has lifted the spirits of many. Thank you both for making the world a happier place.

3 Affirmation

"I express myself verbally and creatively and live a joyful life."

Number 4: The Dedicated Worker

Number 4s are the dedicated hard workers of the world who take their responsibilities seriously. Due to their stable, practical, and reliable natures, they're often the pillars of the workplace, community, and family. They're the ones we depend on to keep the rest of us in line. With a tendency to see things as either black or white, 4s have good old-fashioned values and morals and easily know right from wrong. They're always true to their word and are conscious of doing the honorable thing. If they commit to something, they'll follow through and won't let anyone down—unless it's beyond their control.

Because 4s work systematically and methodically, thrive on routine, and prefer to be in control of their environment, they often find it hard to adapt to change. This is why becoming more flexible and adaptable is one of their major life lessons. Emotional, physical, and financial stability is vital to their well-being, and their "pay now, play later" mentality helps them succeed. Number 4s provide stability and order where there is disharmony and chaos, and their precise and authoritative guidance pulls everyone in line.

Disciplined and determined, 4s persevere through adversity by using a step-by-step approach to achieve their goals. Life can be frustrating for 4s when they are held back by limitations; however, their lesson is to see the light at the end of the tunnel and use their courage, strength, and tenacity to make it through. Once they accept—and let go of—the things they cannot change, rather than fight against the natural flow, their obstacles disintegrate so they are able to move forward with their lives. Even though 4s can be controlling, intolerant, judgmental, and emotionally withdrawn at times (unless they have an emotional astrology chart or other, emotional Core Numbers such as 2, 3, 6, or 9), they're the most honest and hardworking of all the numbers. Yes, they can be inflexible, stubborn, and abrupt, but they are assets to us all. If everyone were as reliable, responsible, and law-abiding as the number 4s, the world would be a much better place.

4's Strengths

- Hardworking
- Practical
- Grounded
- Stable
- Reliable
- Conscientious
- Organized
- Focused

- Disciplined
- Persistent

4's Weaknesses

- Intolerant
- Judgmental
- Critical
- Stubborn
- Narrow-minded
- Inflexible
- Pessimistic
- Controlling
- Pedantic
- Emotionally closed

Life Lessons

The major life lessons number 4s need to learn in this lifetime are:

- To persist through adversity
- To embrace and surrender to change
- To be flexible and adaptable
- To think outside the box
- To embrace gradual progress
- To build a stable foundation
- To express affection and emotion
- To make time for fun and relaxation

Astrological Equivalent

Most astrologers believe that the astrological equivalent to number 4 is Taurus; however, some feel that it also resonates with Capricorn and Virgo.

Suitable Career Choices

CEO, manager, business owner, personal assistant, editor, auditor, bookkeeper, accountant, administrator, de-clutterer, physician, technician, police or military officer, life coach, personal trainer, analyst, landscaper, architect, urban planner, farmer, lawyer, event planner, executive, business consultant, proofreader, teacher, author, building superintendent or construction worker, banking or finance professional.

Compatibility

Number 4s are said to be most compatible with numbers 1, 2, 4, 6, 7, 8, 11/2, 22/4, and 33/6.

4 Life Path Number

As a 4 Life Path, you're here to walk the path of the Dedicated Worker so you can bring stability, organization, and order to your family, your community, and/or the world. You're the pillar of the community, workplace, and family, with the discipline and tenacity to get things done. You prefer to live a balanced and organized life and may struggle to adapt to change; therefore, life will encourage you to be more adaptable and flexible and to think outside the box. At times you may feel as if life is just one big obstacle after another, but if you choose to see the glass half-full and focus on the positives, you'll be rewarded for your efforts. Persistence and a positive mind-set are the keys to your success. As a 4 Life

Path, you're fulfilling your life purpose when you use a step-by-step process to build a secure and stable foundation.

4 Destiny Number

As a 4 Destiny, you're destined to be a Dedicated Worker who brings stability, organization, and order to the world. Your life's mission is to manage and organize others—whether it be in your personal life or career. You're a natural facilitator who knows what needs to be done to get results. You're also a gifted delegator who can bring out the best in others. Security and stability are vital to your well-being; however, you must guard against becoming a workaholic. You must put time aside for relaxation and fun in order to remain centered and balanced. Regardless of how challenging your life may be at times, when you persevere through adversity, your efforts will eventually pay off.

4 Soul Number

As a 4 Soul, you long to be a Dedicated Worker who brings stability, organization, and order to your family, workplace, and community. In your heart of hearts, all your soul wants is to obtain financial, emotional, and physical stability so you can live a secure life. As a 4 Soul, you appreciate (and are motivated by) honesty, commitment, and responsibility. To you, truth, practicality, and reality are far more important than superficiality, glitz, and glamour. As you work toward creating a solid foundation for your future, you fulfill your heart's desire.

4 Personality Number

As a 4 Personality, you may be perceived as being a down-to-earth, hard worker whom others can rely on. You come across as responsible, reliable, and honest, and someone to be trusted. People may turn to you for guidance because they value your expertise and judgment. Even those who view you as standoffish, stubborn, and tactless will come to you for assistance in their times of need.

4 Maturity Number

With a 4 Maturity Number, life is steering you toward becoming a Dedicated Worker who brings stability, organization, and order to your family, workplace, and community. Your life's goal is to build a solid foundation for your future and to commit yourself to your dreams. As you mature, you'll find yourself becoming more organized, disciplined, and focused with respect to achieving your goals. A 4 Maturity Number also indicates an ability to persevere through adversity and improve your financial situation.

4 Birth Day Number (4th, 13th, 22nd, and 31st)

As a 4 Birth Day, you're gifted with the ability to stubbornly push through in order to overcome your challenges. Your discipline, determination, and focus enable you to attain your goals. Even though you may have trouble communicating your feelings, you'd do anything for those you love and make a loyal partner and friend. You have good old-fashioned values and morals and are conscientious about doing the right thing.

4 Current Name Number

A 4 Current Name enhances your ability to persevere through adversity to achieve your goals. It also enables you to make a commitment and dedicate yourself to a project, relationship, or dream. This number will help you be more organized, disciplined, economical, and focused so you can build a solid foundation for your future.

4 Karmic Lesson Number

Throughout the course of this life, you'll need to adopt the characteristics of number 4 by being more responsible, disciplined, and focused. There will be times when you'll need to work hard to build a stable emotional and financial foundation and to put your ideas into physical form. This karmic lesson will force you to be more practical and organized in your everyday life.

4 Checklist

To determine whether you're fully embracing your "4-ness," ask yourself these questions:

- *Am I a leader, manager, or organizer of others?*
- *Do I help others get their lives in order?*
- *Am I working hard to build a solid foundation for my future?*
- *Am I using a step-by-step process to achieve my goals?*

4 Example

Media entrepreneur and talk-show host Oprah Winfrey (1-29-1954) is a classic example of a 4 Life Path with a Master Number 29/11/2 Birth Day and Master Number 11/2 Maturity Number who is fulfilling her life purpose as a Dedicated Worker and Inspirational Teacher, raising awareness on planet Earth. Born into a life of poverty, Oprah has had her fair share of adversity and obstacles to overcome. Due to the tenacity and dedication of her number 4, she has managed to see the light at the end of the tunnel and gradually build her media empire one step at a time. Due to her hard work and perseverance, today she's one of the most successful and influential people in the world. Thanks for raising the spiritual awareness of mainstream society, Oprah! You've certainly contributed to making the world a better place. And with your Master

11/2 Maturity Number, your best is yet to come! *Whoop-whoop—* bring it on, girl!

4 Affirmation

"I promote organization and order and make the world a better place."

NUMBER 5: THE FREEDOM-LOVING ADVENTURER

Number 5s are the Freedom-Loving Adventurers of the world who are always on the move. They enjoy visiting new places, meeting new people, learning new things, and partaking in exciting new experiences. They're natural-born detectives with curious minds who lead colorful and changeable lives. Even though they're gifted communicators who love to teach, speak, and promote what interests them, their short attention spans and need for constant mental stimulation can make them easily bored and distracted. They are gifted salespeople, networkers, and teachers who know a little about a lot of things.

Number 5s need the space, time, and freedom to do what they want, when they want to do it. Depending on their astrology profile and the other numbers in their chart, they may avoid responsibility and commitment. Multitalented and clever, 5s have a diverse range of aptitudes and abilities; however, without discipline and focus or the presence of grounding numbers or astrology signs in their chart, they can fail to develop their full potential. These unconventional risk takers think outside the box and are magnetic and attractive to almost everyone they meet. They're here to squeeze as many experiences as they possibly can into this life—and to have a good time while they're doing it.

Number 5s are natural entertainers who can relate to those of all walks of life, from the cleaner to the CEO. They make friends easily, and people are fascinated by their stories. They're highly intelligent and very quick learners, but their boredom often causes them to skim the surface rather than plumb genuine depths of experience. In their quest to avoid the humdrum of every-day life, 5s who are living as their lower selves can be addicted to chaos, drama, and the sensual pleasures of life. Sex, alcohol, food, gambling, overspending, excessive exercising, or obsessive behavior can sometimes be used as a form of escapism. Therefore, temperance, moderation, and exercising restraint are the keys to their success. These enthusiastic and unconventional motivators inspire us to be free and to think outside the box.

5's Strengths

- Adaptable
- Magnetic
- Progressive
- Clever
- Multitalented
- Resourceful
- Courageous
- Adventurous
- Resilient
- Enthusiastic

5's Weaknesses

- Prone to addiction
- Unreliable
- Inclined to exaggerate
- Dishonest
- Scattered
- Irresponsible

- Intolerant
- Noncommittal
- Restless
- Inconsistent

Life Lessons

The major life lessons number 5 needs to learn in this lifetime are:

- To learn to use their freedom constructively
- To embrace temperance and moderation
- To plan and prioritize
- To focus and commit
- To achieve a depth of experience
- To be honest and authentic
- To eliminate unnecessary drama
- To be patient and tolerant

Astrological Equivalent

Most astrologers believe that the astrological equivalent to number 5 is Gemini; however, some feel that it also resonates with Aquarius.

Suitable Career Choices

Travel consultant; travel guide; airline worker; event planner; reporter; public speaker; advertising, marketing, or sales consultant; promoter; communications or media professional; detective; teacher; therapist; hairstylist; cosmetologist; writer; sales representative; personal trainer; life coach; publicist; journalist; receptionist; television or radio presenter; hospitality professional (anything to do with people—5s often work in a variety of roles).

Compatibility

Number 5s are said to be most compatible with numbers 1, 3, 5, 7, and 9.

5 Life Path Number

As a 5 Life Path, you're here to walk the path of the Freedom-Loving Adventurer who lives life to the fullest and makes the most of every experience. Life is meant to be explored, and you were born to try everything it has to offer—provided that you do so in moderation. Even though you need to be free to be yourself without any restrictions and limitations, you must learn to be responsible and use your freedom wisely. Your varied talents and interests make you good at many different things, but in order to maintain a stable career, you need to feel stimulated and challenged through a variety of tasks, clients, or roles. As a 5 Life Path, you're fulfilling your life purpose when you experience as much as you can in this lifetime and teach others what you've learned.

5 Destiny Number

As a 5 Destiny, you're destined to be a Freedom-Loving Adventurer who lives life to the fullest and makes the most of every experience. Your life's mission is to experience as much as you can in this life and teach others what you've learned. You may promote a product, service, or philosophy that has helped you in your life; or you may simply teach your loved ones the life lessons you have learned. As a 5 Destiny, you're a gifted communicator, messenger, and promoter who loves to "spread the word." If you're passionate about something, you were born to communicate your findings. You're a gifted salesperson, networker, and teacher, so put your talents to good use.

5 Soul Number

As a 5 Soul, you long to be a Freedom-Loving Adventurer who lives life to the fullest and makes the most of every experience. In your heart of hearts, all your soul wants is for you to be free to be yourself and live without restrictions and limitations while embracing that freedom constructively. As a 5 Soul, you're motivated by new experiences, people, travel, variety, excitement, and adventure. When you meet new people, visit new places, and learn and experience new things, you fulfill your heart's desire.

5 Personality Number

As a 5 Personality, you may be perceived as a dynamic and confident go-getter who can talk to anybody about anything. You could come across as outgoing, magnetic, and charming, but may also appear easily distracted or bored. You have the gift of gab, and people are usually drawn to your energy. They may find you inspirational and entertaining, yet unpredictable at the same time. Try to be honest, present, and authentic in order to make the best impression.

5 Maturity Number

With a 5 Maturity Number, life is steering you toward becoming a Freedom-Loving Adventurer who lives life to the fullest and makes the most of every experience. Your life's goal is to learn as much as you can about this world and pass your findings on to others. As you mature, you'll find yourself becoming more outgoing, adventurous, and daring. A 5 Maturity Number also indicates many new places to visit and new people to meet. There will be no slowing you down, as there are countless exciting experiences to come.

5 Birth Day Number (5th, 14th, and 23rd)

As a 5 Birth Day, you're gifted with the ability to communicate effectively with others. You'd make an excellent teacher, consultant, promoter, salesperson, writer, or reporter. You're bright, witty, and clever, with a knack for learning new things. Even though you have a variety of interests and talents, you can become easily bored and distracted. Discipline, moderation, and balance are the keys to your success.

5 Current Name Number

A 5 Current Name enhances your ability to communicate effectively with others and promote a product, service, or message. It also enables you to be more flexible and versatile so you can adapt more easily to change. This number will help you become more adventurous and daring so you can take calculated risks and think outside the box. This is the number of the adventurer and communicator.

5 Karmic Lesson Number

Throughout the course of this life, you'll need to adopt the characteristics of number 5 by becoming more flexible and adaptable to change. There will be times when you'll need to step outside your comfort zone to live a fuller life and take a risk without any guarantee of the outcome. This karmic lesson will force you to communicate more effectively with others and grow through personal experience.

5 Checklist

To determine whether you're fully embracing your "5-ness," ask yourself these questions:

- *Am I experiencing as much as I can in this life?*
- *Am I making the most of every opportunity and experience?*
- *Do I communicate what I've learned to help others improve their lives?*
- *Am I a messenger who teaches and promotes what I believe in?*

5 Example

Actress and international sex symbol Angelina Jolie (6-4-1975) is a classic example of a 5 Life Path fulfilling her life purpose as a Freedom-Loving Adventurer. Her magnetic and charismatic personality draws people in, and she oozes sex appeal and danger (typical 5 traits). Her past drug addiction and sexual experimentation were typical examples of a 5 living as its lower self in search of the next high. However, these days (due to her 6 Destiny and 6 Soul) she is living by her higher ideals and is stimulated by her family and a variety of humanitarian pursuits that she passionately supports. As a Goodwill Ambassador for the United Nations High Commissioner for Refugees, Angelina now channels the energy of her 5 to create freedom and well-being for others. Way to go, Angelina! Keep up the good work.

5 Affirmation

*"I embrace my freedom to explore
every opportunity and life experience."*

NUMBER 6: THE RESPONSIBLE CAREGIVER

Number 6s are the Responsible Caregivers of the world, and their greatest gift is their ability to nurture others with love. They're natural counselors and solid advisors who go above and beyond the call of duty to offer a helping hand. Relationships are their number one priority, for they are natural parents and providers who dedicate themselves to love. Whether it's for the sake of romantic love or the love of family, children, or friends, 6s will often sacrifice their own needs to put others first. They are often creatively or musically gifted, or are passionate lovers of music.

Number 6s like to take responsibility for everybody and everything in their lives; however, in their quest to do right by everyone, they often end up becoming martyrs. They often feel as if they're not being, giving, doing, or achieving "enough." In their mission to improve people's lives, they can take responsibility too far by interfering excessively. Even though their intentions come from the heart and they're only trying to help, they need to find a balance between *giving* and *receiving, helping* and *interfering,* and *assisting* and *enabling* the people in their lives. Number 6s are here to learn that they cannot help others who aren't willing to help themselves. In other words, 6s must discover that they can lead a horse to water, but they can't make it drink.

This number governs love, friendship, parenting, marriage, and divorce, and 6s are here to learn lessons in these areas. However, that doesn't mean every 6 is going to marry and divorce, or conceive children. Idealists and perfectionists, 6s have high standards for themselves and others; therefore, they can find it hard to accept, let go, and move on from misfortune, their own mistakes, and the imperfections in the world. They strive to be their best and want others to do the same, but they must learn that perfect people, relationships, and experiences simply don't exist. Despite their extremely idealistic views and values, the nurturing love of the 6s—the parents, lovers, and healers—is desperately needed in this world.

6's Strengths

- Generous
- Responsible
- Nurturing
- Loving
- Creative
- Supportive
- Wise
- Conscientious
- Sympathetic
- Dependable

6's Weaknesses

- Self-righteous
- Interfering
- Critical
- Perfectionistic
- Bossy
- Martyrish
- Jealous
- Self-critical
- Unrealistic
- Prone to worry

Life Lessons

The major life lessons number 6s need to learn in this lifetime are:

- To love and appreciate themselves
- To balance giving and receiving
- To be responsible for others and themselves
- To know how to say no
- To come to terms with imperfection
- To accept, let go, and move on
- To respect others' boundaries
- To recognize love in its many forms

Astrological Equivalent

Most astrologers believe that the astrological equivalent to number 6 is Libra; however, some feel it also resonates with Cancer and Taurus.

Suitable Career Choices

Hairstylist, fashion or interior designer, florist, psychiatrist, therapist, teacher, healer, chef, decorator, customer-service representative, nurse, caregiver, alternative therapist, child-care professional, stay-at-home mom or dad, artist, landscaper, color consultant, musician, actor, model, massage therapist, makeup artist, life coach, personal trainer, midwife, doctor or health professional, recruitment consultant, career counselor, cosmetologist.

Compatibility

Number 6s are said to be most compatible with numbers 2, 3, 4, 6, 8, 9, 11/2, 22/4, and 33/6.

6 Life Path Number

As a 6 Life Path, you're here to walk the path of the Responsible Caregiver who serves, supports, and nurtures others with love. Whether you're responsible for your family, friends, children, clients, or work colleagues, you enjoy going out of your way to help others improve their lives. You may work in a creative or service-based career catering to people's needs; however, you'll need to attend to your home life along with your career to attain overall balance in your life. You like to do the right thing and are generous with your money, attention, and time; there are times, though, when you may feel that your efforts aren't reciprocated. As a 6 Life Path, you're fulfilling your life purpose when you provide unconditional love to those who cross your path, without neglecting your own needs in the process.

6 Destiny Number

As a 6 Destiny, you're destined to be a Responsible Caregiver who serves, supports, and nurtures others with love. Your life's mission is to be of service to those in need, without neglecting your own self-care. You may be the pillar of your family, community, workplace, or circle of friends; and you may work in a creative or service-based career. You make a good counselor and advisor, and people open up to you and trust you with their personal information. As a 6 Destiny, you're destined to experience love, beauty, and creativity in every possible form. You have an enormous capacity to heal, so put your talents to good use.

6 Soul Number

As a 6 Soul, you long to be a Responsible Caregiver who serves, supports, and nurtures others with love. In your heart of hearts, all your soul wants is to bring love, beauty, and harmony into the world so everybody can feel happy, loved, and healed. As a 6 Soul, you're motivated by beauty, love, family, relationships, and being of service to others. Every time you beautify the world, offer a shoulder to cry on, and provide unconditional love, you fulfill your heart's desire.

6 Personality Number

As a 6 Personality, you may be perceived as someone others can turn to during times of need. You come across as wise, supportive, and caring; however, because you can't say no, you may get taken advantage of or taken for granted. People see you as someone who takes his or her responsibilities seriously and likes to do the right thing. Even those who view you as judgmental, meddling, or bossy will tell you their deep, dark secrets and appreciate your advice.

6 Maturity Number

With a 6 Maturity Number, life is steering you toward becoming a Responsible Caregiver who serves, supports, and nurtures others with love. Your life's goal is to provide unconditional love to those who cross your path, without neglecting your own needs in the process. As you mature, you'll find yourself expanding your capacity to love and becoming more involved with community, business, and family affairs. You may even be drawn to a creative or service-based career later in life. A 6 Maturity Number can also indicate meaningful friendships and relationships to come, along with opportunities to improve your finances and advance your career.

6 Birth Day Number (6th, 15th, and 24th)

As a 6 Birth Day, you're gifted with the ability to love, nurture, teach, counsel, support, and heal others—whether it's your partner, children, family, clients, work colleagues, or friends. You'd do anything for someone in need, but you must define your personal limits and boundaries and find the balance between giving and receiving. You're sympathetic, loving, and kind, with a gift for healing hearts, but you often feel guilty for not being, doing, giving, or achieving enough.

6 Current Name Number

A 6 Current Name enhances your ability to love, heal, nurture, parent, create, teach, and serve. It also enables you to be more sympathetic and compassionate, and form meaningful connections with others. This number will help you be a good parent, partner, counselor, or teacher. This is also the number of the healer, artist, and musician.

6 Karmic Lesson Number

Throughout the course of this life, you'll need to adopt the characteristics of number 6 by being more sympathetic and dutiful toward others. There will be times when you'll need to take responsibility for them and cater to their needs, sacrificing your own desires in the process. This karmic lesson will force you to open up to love and establish authentic relationships. It will also teach you to take responsibility for your actions and accept imperfection in yourself, others, and the world.

6 Checklist

To determine whether you're fully embracing your "6-ness," ask yourself these questions:

- *Do I offer a helping hand to those in need?*

- *Am I the pillar of my family, community, or circle of friends?*

- *Do I offer my love, time, guidance, and support when needed?*

- *Do I use my creative gifts to beautify my life and my home?*

6 Example

World-renowned psychiatrist and author Elisabeth Kübler-Ross (7-8-1926) is a classic example of a 6 Life Path (using the reducing-down and adding-down methods) or a Master Number 33/6 Life Path (using the adding-across method), who fulfilled her life purpose as a Responsible Caregiver by serving, healing, supporting, and nurturing others with love. Elisabeth wrote the book *On Death and Dying,* which identifies the five stages of grief, to assist people through the loss of loved ones. During the course of her life as a 6 Life Path, she experienced marriage, motherhood, healing, teaching, and divorce—all typical 6 experiences. On top of that, she also founded a healing center for the dying and their families. Now you can't get any more "6" than that! Thank you, Elisabeth, for your loving dedication to others! May you rest in peace.

6 Affirmation

"I counsel, serve, and heal others and myself with love."

NUMBER 7: THE CONTEMPLATIVE TRUTH SEEKER

Number 7s are the Contemplative Truth Seekers of the world who need quiet time alone to ponder the meaning of life and become a specialist in their craft. Whether their alone time is spent meditating, relaxing, thinking, analyzing, studying, reading, gardening, or just puttering around, it is vital to their well-being and helps keep them centered. It's important that partners and associates of 7s understand this about this number so they don't take their need for time by themselves personally. They're not as social and outgoing as the other numbers (unless they're a 34/7 Life Path; have an outgoing astrology chart; or have outgoing Core Numbers such as 1, 3, and 5). Instead, they're the scholars, philosophers, and analysts of the world who love to learn and who need their space to "just be."

Number 7s are the seekers of knowledge, wisdom, and understanding. Even though they were born to discover the secrets and mysteries of the Universe and to find their spiritual truth, they're skeptical by nature and form their beliefs solely through personal experience. Despite 7 being a "spiritual" number, some 7s are pessimistic atheists who believe that there is no spiritual truth. Either way, 7s are highly perceptive and intuitive and are good judges of character who can see through people and situations. They won't open up to just anyone, and they don't wear their hearts on their sleeves. They're private and distrusting by nature, so if you want to get to know them, you'll need to earn their confidence and trust.

Time in nature and the outdoors is vital to a 7's well-being— especially in or around water (although some have a fear of water). Even though they can feel socially uncomfortable and awkward at times, 7s are talented problem solvers and strategists who can excel in metaphysics, science, psychology, philosophy, research, analytics, education, health, and technology (especially computers and IT). Despite their cynical and pessimistic nature, they make trustworthy partners and friends. Number 7s are the ones to thank for many of the technological and scientific breakthroughs in the world. Thank you, 7s, for much of the psychological, spiritual, and scientific advancement on planet Earth.

7's Strengths

- Independent
- Intuitive
- Analytical
- Intellectual
- Deep
- Insightful
- Inquisitive
- Contemplative
- Technically oriented
- Philosophical

7's Weaknesses

- Secretive
- Untrusting
- Pessimistic
- Cynical
- Emotionally closed
- Defensive
- Skeptical
- Withdrawn
- Intolerant
- Perfectionistic

Life Lessons

The major life lessons number 7s need to learn in this lifetime are:

- To discover their spiritual truth
- To be open and trusting of others
- To involve themselves in life
- To communicate their emotions
- To embrace imperfection
- To be open-minded
- To be patient and tolerant
- To have hope and faith

Astrological Equivalent

Most astrologers believe that the astrological equivalent to number 7 is Pisces; however, some feel that it also resonates with Scorpio.

Suitable Career Choices

Researcher, analyst, IT consultant, philosopher, psychologist, therapist, inventor, reporter, writer, scientist, engineer, computer programmer, web designer, technical or health consultant, accountant, clairvoyant, healer, spiritual teacher, doctor, travel agent, alternative therapist, physical therapist, nutritionist, explorer, journalist, private investigator, executive, musician, mathematician.

Compatibility

Number 7s are said to be most compatible with numbers 1, 4, 5, 7, 9, 11/2, and 22/4.

7 Life Path Number

As a 7 Life Path, you're here to walk the path of the Contemplative Truth Seeker who uncovers the secrets and mysteries of the Universe and finds your spiritual truth. Whether you consider yourself a spiritual person or not, life will send you food for thought to open up your mind. Unless you're a 34/7 Life Path; have an "outgoing" astrology chart; or have numbers 1, 3, and 5 in your chart, you may feel different, withdrawn, or lonely at times and wish you could reach out to others, although you're not quite sure how. As a seeker of knowledge, wisdom, and understanding, you may be drawn to metaphysics and personal development. This is an area where you could excel and build a successful career. As with any career you choose, focus and specialization are the keys to your success. As a 7 Life Path, you're fulfilling your life purpose when you uncover the truth and discover the meaning of life.

7 Destiny Number

As a 7 Destiny, you're destined to be a Contemplative Truth Seeker who discovers the secrets and mysteries of the Universe and finds your spiritual truth. Your life's mission is to reveal answers to the big questions: *Who am I? Where am I going?* and *What is the meaning of life?* You may be drawn to psychology and other fields related to the workings of the mind, or you may be a talented researcher, programmer, or analyst. As a 7 Destiny, you're a gifted seeker and teacher, so put your talents to good use.

7 Soul Number

As a 7 Soul, you long to be a Contemplative Truth Seeker who discovers the secrets and mysteries of the Universe and finds your spiritual truth. In your heart of hearts, all your soul wants is to get to the bottom of things to see what lies beneath. You may achieve this with science, metaphysics, technology, psychology, philosophy, religion, or other academic pursuits. As a 7 Soul, you're motivated by knowledge, wisdom, and understanding. Every time you search beyond the physical world for answers, you fulfill your heart's desire.

7 Personality Number

As a 7 Personality, you may be perceived as intelligent, mysterious, and intriguing. Some may see you as a cryptic puzzle they'd like to figure out. You likely come across as an introspective deep thinker who has a unique philosophy about life. Even those who view you as guarded, sarcastic, and reserved are drawn to your intuitive insights and wisdom. By having a little more trust and faith in others, you will make your best impression. Try to be less closed-off and self-protective so people can get to know you.

7 Maturity Number

With a 7 Maturity Number, life is steering you toward becoming a Contemplative Truth Seeker who discovers the secrets and mysteries of the Universe. Your life's goal is to raise your conscious awareness and enhance your connection with the Divine. As you mature, you may find yourself needing time alone to study or to focus on your personal or spiritual development. You may wish to explore philosophy, psychology, metaphysics, science, technology, or alternative health. A 7 Maturity Number also indicates an ability to attain a deeper level of knowledge and wisdom and become a specialist in your craft.

7 Birth Day Number (7th, 16th, and 25th)

As a 7 Birth Day, you're gifted with the ability to achieve great depths of understanding and awareness. You're extremely intuitive and perceptive and can easily enhance your psychic abilities with regular meditation and training. You're a private person whose trust must be earned before you'll offer the key to your heart. You need a lot of time alone to process life and revitalize your soul. Quiet time in nature and the outdoors is vital to your well-being.

7 Current Name Number

A 7 Current Name enhances your ability to retain information through research or study. It also enables you to achieve great depths of understanding and awareness, both academically and spiritually. This number will help you become a talented researcher, teacher, and analyzer of information, especially in the sciences and the fields of metaphysics, philosophy, psychology, and technology.

7 Karmic Lesson Number

Throughout the course of this life, you'll need to adopt the characteristics of number 7 by finding a spiritual faith from which you can discover your truth. There will be times when you'll need to put extra effort into mastering your craft and becoming a specialist in your field; an optimistic attitude is the key to achieving your goals. This karmic lesson will force you to put trust in yourself, others, and the Divine, and to look beyond the physical world to discover the meaning of life.

7 Checklist

To determine whether you're fully embracing your "7-ness," ask yourself these questions:

- *Am I on a quest to discover the meaning of life?*
- *Am I working on my personal development?*
- *Am I searching for my spiritual truth?*

- *Do I make time for contemplation, meditation, and prayer?*

7 Example

Physician, scientist, and internationally best-selling author Deepak Chopra, M.D. (10-22-1946), is a classic example of a 7 Life Path and a Master Number 22/4 Birth Day fulfilling his life purpose as a Contemplative Truth Seeker and Master Builder who has discovered the secrets and mysteries of the Universe and is building something of benefit for humankind. Dr. Chopra has written more than 60 books on mind-body medicine and healing and has established the Chopra Center for Wellbeing in Carlsbad, California. In 2009 he founded the Chopra Foundation, with a mission to advance the cause of mind-body-spirit healing, education, and research through fund-raising on behalf of select projects. Hooray, Deepak—you're a legend, and we love you!

7 Affirmation

"I discover my spiritual truth and improve my quality of life."

NUMBER 8: THE BUSINESS-MINDED LEADER

Number 8s are the Business-Minded Leaders of the world who are usually drawn to self-employment or positions of authority. As talented problem solvers, they enjoy the thrill of a challenge and are driven to succeed. Their strength, determination, and vision—combined with their good judgment and practicality—enable them to reach, and often exceed, their goals. When they live by their higher ideals, they can be extremely successful in business. But when they have a negative attitude about life and money, they often struggle financially. If they can overcome their tendency to worry, they have much potential for success.

Eight is the number of money, career, and manifestation, so 8s must learn to adopt an attitude of abundance and have a healthy relationship with their finances. They must also rise above their tendency to define themselves and/or others through money, image, status, or power. Number 8s have the ability to manifest wealth and abundance, provided that they live by their higher ideals and balance the material and spiritual worlds. If they're dishonest, miserly, manipulative, or greedy, they can struggle financially or experience a reversal of fortune. This is because 8 is the also the number of karmic balance, where 8s will reap what they've sown. They cannot get away with anything, because they are governed by the Law of Cause and Effect.

But not all 8s are focused on money, status, and career. Others are dealing with issues relating to personal power—either being afraid of it or misusing it to manipulate and control. Some need to overcome their tendency to intimidate and overpower, while others need to learn not to give their power away. Regardless, 8s must rise above their internal power struggles in order to succeed. Despite their abrupt and businesslike manner, their ability to organize, lead, and inspire is an asset to us all.

8's Strengths

- Organized

- Authoritative

- Pioneering

- Self-motivated

- Dependable

- Tenacious

- Strong

- Driven

- Fair

- Hardworking

8's Weaknesses

- Workaholic
- Egotistical
- Domineering
- Manipulative
- Greedy
- Prone to worry
- Poverty-conscious
- Intolerant
- Superficial
- Intimidating

Life Lessons

The major life lessons number 8s need to learn in this lifetime are:

- To balance the material and spiritual worlds
- To recognize the illusory nature of the material world
- To adopt an attitude of abundance
- To reclaim their personal power
- To temper power with respect
- To lead alongside others
- To become aware of a higher purpose
- To live with honesty and integrity

Astrological Equivalent

Most astrologers believe that the astrological equivalent to number 8 is Capricorn; however, some feel that it also resonates with Leo and Taurus.

Suitable Career Choices

Business owner, independent contractor, manager, supervisor, team leader, banker, financial analyst, business advisor, real-estate broker, property developer, surgeon, lawyer, politician, executive, administrator, marketing professional, life coach, consultant, project manager. (Some 8s prefer not to work at all, while others work so hard that they're able to retire early. Occasionally 8s may live off a wealthy partner or family who supports them.)

Compatibility

Number 8s are said to be most compatible with numbers 4, 6, 8, 22/4, and 33/6.

8 Life Path Number

As an 8 Life Path, you're here to walk the path of the Business-Minded Leader who lives by your higher ideals and exudes an attitude of abundance. You have a powerful mind that enables you to manifest whatever you focus your attention on the most—so focus on your dreams rather than your fears. As an 8, you can generate wealth, power, and abundance, but you must live with honesty and integrity at all times to make your dreams come true. As a gifted leader, you can rise to a position of authority in the workplace or succeed in self-employment; however, your motivation and mind-set are the keys to your success. When you rise above whatever causes you to feel victimized, you can reach your highest potential and improve your quality of life. As an 8 Life

Path, you're fulfilling your life purpose when you're generous and empowered and have a healthy relationship with money.

8 Destiny Number

As an 8 Destiny, you're destined to be a Business-Minded Leader who lives by your higher ideals and leads, manages, or assists others who lack your capability and strength. Your life's mission is to adopt an attitude of abundance while balancing the material and spiritual worlds. During the course of this life, you're destined to reclaim your personal power and utilize your creative ability to manifest your dreams. You must also overcome your tendency to measure your own and others' success through physical appearance, material accumulation, wealth, status, or power. As an 8 Destiny, you're a gifted organizer and achiever, so put your talents to good use.

8 Soul Number

As an 8 Soul, you long to be a Business-Minded Leader who lives by your higher ideals and exudes an attitude of abundance. In your heart of hearts, all your soul wants is to feel balanced, empowered, and abundant in your personal life and work. As an 8 Soul, you're motivated by responsibility, goals, and challenges—especially within your career. You may wish to be self-employed, and thrive on leading others toward achieving a common goal. Every time you hold a vision in your mind and bring it to fruition with determination and courage, you fulfill your heart's desire.

8 Personality Number

As an 8 Personality, you may be perceived as someone who is confident, competent, and strong. You often come across as the person in charge who takes control of a situation and gets the job done. You take pride in your appearance, and it shows; however, to make the best impression, try not to be overly concerned with your image, status, and power. Even those who view you as intimidating, domineering, or conceited will trust your vision and judgment and willingly follow your lead.

8 Maturity Number

With an 8 Maturity Number, life is steering you toward becoming a Business-Minded Leader who lives by your higher ideals and leads, manages, or organizes people and projects. Your life's goal is to balance your personal power and adopt an attitude of abundance. As you mature, you'll find yourself becoming more focused on your career and driven to achieve your goals. An 8 Maturity Number also indicates an opportunity to rise to a position of authority or to begin a business endeavor of your own. If you live with integrity, have a healthy relationship with money, and adopt a positive mind-set, there is much potential for success.

8 Birth Day Number (8th, 17th, and 26th)

As an 8 Birth Day, you're gifted with the ability to lead, manage, and organize people and projects. You're courageous, strong, and determined, but you must use your influence and power for the greater good, rather than just for yourself. You have the potential to attain material wealth and success, but you must learn that true success cannot be measured by power, money, image, or status. Once you see the illusion in the material world, you will make your dreams come true.

8 Current Name Number

An 8 Current Name enhances your ability to focus, lead, achieve, and manifest abundance. It also enables you to have a

81

better understanding of the business and financial worlds. Provided you have a positive mind-set and a healthy relationship with money, this number will help you build a successful career and reclaim your personal power in every area of your life.

8 Karmic Lesson Number

Throughout the course of this life, you'll need to adopt the characteristics of number 8 by reclaiming your personal power and exuding an attitude of abundance. There will be times when you'll need to overcome your victim mentality and rise above your tendency to define yourself and/or others through money, image, status, and power. This karmic lesson will force you to overcome your need to manipulate and control people and your environment. It will also encourage you to live with honesty and integrity.

8 Checklist

To determine whether you're fully embracing your "8-ness," ask yourself these questions:

- *Am I an organizer, manager, or leader of others?*
- *Am I standing in my full personal power or taking steps toward feeling empowered?*
- *Do I have a positive mind-set and a healthy relationship with money?*
- *Am I using my creative mind to manifest my dreams?*

8 Example

Lifestyle guru and entrepreneur Martha Stewart (8-3-1941) is a classic example of an 8 Life Path using the creativity of her 3 Birth Day to fulfill her life purpose as a Business-Minded Leader and Self-Expressive Creative. Over the past three decades, she has risen to a position of authority, achieved wealth and abundance, and built a successful business empire through expertise in a variety of creative endeavors ranging from cooking, decorating, and writing to television hosting. Although she experienced a reversal of fortune in 2002 (a common 8 experience), which resulted in a prison sentence due to insider stock trading, the tenacity of her number 8 enabled her to rebuild her career and be successful once again. As Martha has learned from personal experience, it pays to be honest at all times when you're working with the karmic 8.

8 Affirmation

"I adopt an attitude of abundance and reclaim my personal power."

NUMBER 9: THE COMPASSIONATE HUMANITARIAN

Number 9s are the Compassionate Humanitarians of the world who like to fight for the underdog and make the world a better place. They're extremely generous, sympathetic, and kind, and they feel the pain of others. It's not uncommon to see them fighting for a cause or donating their time, attention, or money to the underprivileged, animals, or the environment. Not all 9s are selfless and compassionate, though. In fact, most grow *into* becoming Compassionate Humanitarians through their life lessons and experiences. Even though a willingness to serve lies deep within them, it takes a complete overcoming of their lower selves to bring it to the surface and have it remain there. They reach their potential when they live by their higher ideals, but it's up to them whether they choose to do so.

Many 9s are creative and have a love of the literary, performing, and visual arts. Even those who don't may have a hidden creative talent that can be developed over time. Number 9s tend to excel in writing, designing, painting, acting, dancing, public speaking, and music. Because they're ruled by Mars, the planet of war, they can be extremely sensitive and passionate and may have a volatile temper to match. Many are drawn to a career of service in healing, health, education, the military, philanthropy, or the arts. Even those who reject a life of service are extremely giving, loving, and supportive of their partners, family members, and friends. Number 9s are here to learn tolerance and forgiveness, and to gain an understanding of human suffering.

Number 9s make wonderful parents who put their children first; however, many (but not all) struggle to leave their own family issues behind. Some felt abandoned, misunderstood, or abused, while others felt smothered, overprotected, or controlled. Nevertheless, they must put the past behind them in order to create a harmonious future. As forgiveness is one of their major life lessons, they must also learn to rise above their desire to punish or seek revenge if someone wrongs them. Gifted healers, teachers, and leaders, 9s make the world a better place with their enormous capacity to love.

9's Strengths

- Generous
- Creative
- Sympathetic
- Intuitive
- Wise
- Compassionate
- Multitalented
- Passionate
- Understanding
- Broadminded

9's Weaknesses

- Intolerant
- Impatient
- Unforgiving
- Aggressive
- Temperamental
- Intense
- Moody
- Hypersensitive
- Defensive
- Dramatic

Life Lessons

The major life lessons number 9s need to learn in this lifetime are:

- To be compassionate and tolerant
- To become broadminded
- To live in service to others
- To practice the art of forgiveness
- To accept, let go, and move on
- To work through their family issues
- To express themselves creatively
- To recognize the interconnectedness of humanity

Astrological Equivalent

Most astrologers believe that the astrological equivalent to number 9 is Aries; however, some feel that it also resonates with Scorpio.

Suitable Career Choices

Teacher; artist; writer; doctor; nurse; police or military officer; philanthropist; judge; lawyer; actor; health or education professional; politician; alternative therapist; counselor; social worker; activist; humanitarian; HR or recruitment consultant; publicist; public-relations executive; manager; public speaker; environmentalist; clairvoyant; healer; graphic designer; fashion designer; photographer; or literary, performing, or visual artist.

Compatibility

Number 9s are said to be most compatible with numbers 2, 3, 5, 6, 7, 9, 11/2, 22/4, and 33/6.

9 Life Path Number

As a 9 Life Path, you're here to walk the path of the Compassionate Humanitarian who contributes to making the world a better place. Whether you work in education, health, human resources, law enforcement, child care, or social services—or you simply volunteer for or donate to a cause—you must first accept the imperfection in the world before you can make a change. The perfect place to start is by conquering your prejudice and judgment toward others and accepting the imperfection in yourself. Due to the creative aspect of 9, you may be drawn to acting, designing, public speaking, writing, music, or art. Anything that enables you to use your imagination and express your creative flair is in alignment with your higher purpose. As a 9, you've had your fair share of family drama and other issues to contend with, but when you choose to rise above, forgive, let go, and move on, you're fulfilling your life purpose.

9 Destiny Number

As a 9 Destiny, you're destined to be a Compassionate Humanitarian who contributes to making the world a better place. Your life's mission is to overcome your tendency to judge others and yourself, in order to see humanity in a fairer light. When you forgive yourself and others, and broaden your understanding of human nature, you have much potential for success. As a 9 Destiny, you'll be exposed to many different people, cultures, and walks of life. This will enable you to open your heart and mind as you become more familiar with the diverse world in which you live. You were born with the ability to achieve a high degree of compassion, understanding, and tolerance—so make a difference where you can and put your talents to good use.

9 Soul Number

As a 9 Soul, you long to be a Compassionate Humanitarian who contributes to making the world a better place. In your heart of hearts, all your soul wants is to use every opportunity it is given to promote peace, unity, understanding, forgiveness, and universal love. As a 9 Soul, you're motivated to serve others—whether it's your children, family, friends, or clients . . . or humanity at large, animals, or the environment. You're motivated by creative expression and the pursuit of justice to improve others' lives. Every time you express yourself creatively or do something that serves the greater good, you align yourself with Source and fulfill your heart's desire.

9 Personality Number

As a 9 Personality, you may be perceived as charismatic, passionate, and kind. You likely come across as someone who is generous with money, attention, and time but who can be overly sensitive, emotional, and moody at times. Depending on whether you live by your higher ideals, you may either be viewed as tolerant, compassionate, and understanding or intolerant, impatient, and self-serving. To make the best impression, try to be open-minded, accepting, and humble.

9 Maturity Number

As a 9 Maturity Number, you are being steered toward becoming a Compassionate Humanitarian who contributes to making the world a better place. Your life's goal is to develop a high degree of tolerance, understanding, and compassion toward your fellow man. As you mature, you'll find yourself becoming more involved with community-based endeavors or humanitarian, animal-related, or environmental causes. A 9 Maturity Number also indicates enhanced creative ability, along with increased opportunities to express yourself artistically. You may develop an appreciation for the literary, performing, and visual arts.

9 Birth Day Number (9th, 18th, and 27th)

As a 9 Birth Day, you're gifted with the ability to develop a high degree of understanding, tolerance, and compassion. You're idealistic, creative, and generous with your money, attention, and time, but you may find it hard to forgive others and yourself. You'd do anything for those you love and are passionate about what you believe in, but you must rise above your desire to punish or seek revenge if someone wrongs you. You believe in fairness and justice for all.

9 Current Name Number

A 9 Current Name enhances your creativity and broadens your understanding of people and life. It also enables you to develop a high degree of understanding, compassion, and tolerance. This number will help you serve the greater good, provide unconditional love to all, and support social causes. It will also help you forgive and accept the imperfection in yourself, others, and the world.

9 Karmic Lesson Number

Throughout the course of this life, you'll need to adopt the characteristics of number 9 by being more accepting, tolerant, and compassionate toward others and yourself. There will be times when you'll need to overcome your tendency to judge yourself and other people so that you can be more broadminded and understanding. This karmic lesson will force you to be more generous with your time, money, and attention, and to step outside of your personal vision of the world, in order to be of service to others.

9 Checklist

To determine whether you're fully embracing your "9-ness," ask yourself these questions:

- *Am I drawn to humanitarian pursuits or a career in service?*

- *Am I looking for ways to improve the community or the world?*

- *Am I generous with my money, attention, or time without expecting anything in return?*

- *Am I utilizing my creative talents and abilities?*

9 Example

International best-selling author and spiritual teacher Louise L. Hay (10-8-1926) is a classic example of a 9 Life Path and 8 Birth Day fulfilling her life purpose as a Compassionate Humanitarian and Business-Minded Leader. Her seminal self-help book *You Can Heal Your Life* has sold over 30 million copies worldwide, and her company, Hay House, Inc., is one of the largest publishers of transformational books and products in the world. Louise is a groundbreaking pioneer who has dedicated her life to helping those in need and raising spiritual awareness on planet Earth. Thank you, Louise, for your commitment to humanity and for making the world a better place!

9 Affirmation

*"I am compassionate toward others
and experience compassion in return."*

MASTER NUMBERS

Master Numbers 11/2, 22/4, and 33/6 are higher-octave vibrations of the lower base numbers (2, 4, and 6), and they indicate great potential to attain self-mastery during the course of this life. Those with a Master Number 11/2, 22/4, or 33/6 Life Path, Destiny, Soul, Birth Day, or Maturity Number are old souls who have accumulated much spiritual wisdom in previous lives. Individuals with Master Numbers have free will to decide whether they'll utilize this wisdom in their current lives to help others and contribute to raising the collective consciousness of planet Earth . . . or reject the responsibility and simply live as their base number (2, 4, or 6).

Master Numbers are potent energies vibrating at higher frequencies, and their recipients must overcome the lower tendencies of their base numbers before they can fully harness and utilize the powerful force of the Master Number energy. This intense energy can be destructive when a person hasn't reached the level of maturity and self-confidence to embrace it. Due to their high frequency, Master Numbers can create nerve-related conditions such as anxiety, phobias, extreme sensitivity, and self-doubt—especially in those with a delicate disposition or who already suffer from low self-esteem to begin with. This is why most people revert to the base-number energy until their later years, when they're more confident and grounded, and mature enough to handle the Master Number vibration. Typically, those with strong, confident, and grounded astrology charts and Core Numbers don't experience the same levels of sensitivity and anxiety.

Because we evolve at different rates, some step into their Master Number energy sooner than others, and some don't step into it at all. For many people, life is challenging enough without bringing additional Master Number responsibilities into the mix. This is why it isn't uncommon to see people with Master Numbers living ordinary everyday lives, with minimal concern for the well-being of others or for raising the consciousness of planet Earth. Even so, their Master Number potential is always there, waiting patiently in the background should they wish to step up to the plate and activate it at any time.

Those with Master Numbers are highly evolved souls who know the difference between right and wrong. So they can't get away with anything, because intuitively they know better. Since they're strongly governed by the Law of Cause and Effect, until they learn to live with honesty and integrity, guided by their higher ideals, many will face major life lessons and challenges.

When it comes to the Law of Attraction, those with Master Numbers in their charts are "manifestation maestros" who can actualize their dreams with less effort compared to those without these numbers, particularly when their dreams seek to serve the greater good. However, because the Law of Attraction works both ways and we attract what we focus our attention on the most—be it negative or positive—those with Master Numbers must live in optimism to avoid manifesting their fears.

When recipients have reached the level of maturity and self-confidence to step into their Master Number energy, they have much potential for success—especially when they strive toward self-mastery and serving humankind. While there will be many tests, trials, and tribulations, when they live by their higher ideals, their rewards are nothing short of miraculous. Even though their intuition and extrasensory perception are highly attuned, they must remain centered, balanced, and grounded at all times in order to reach their full psychic potential. All Master Numbers benefit greatly from a healthy diet, regular exercise, spending time in nature, prayer, meditation, yoga, qigong, relaxation techniques, EFT* (Emotional Freedom Technique), conscious breathing, creative visualization, and mindfulness.

Someone with a Master Number who is living up to his or her highest potential—dedicated to transforming lives, attaining spiritual enlightenment, and healing the world—is a powerful force to be reckoned with and is fully supported by the Universe. These individuals have the ability

---

* For more information about EFT, I recommend you read *The Tapping Solution* by Nick Ortner.

to manifest miracles and accomplish great things for humanity, especially since they have chosen to reincarnate to make the world a better place.

Life Lessons
The major life lessons those with Master Numbers need to learn in this lifetime are:

- To understand, love, and believe in themselves
- To utilize their creative power
- To live with honesty and integrity
- To embrace their spirituality and the universal laws
- To utilize their Master Number energy
- To merge the material and spiritual worlds
- To serve humanity and promote unconditional love
- To help raise the collective consciousness of planet Earth

MASTER NUMBER 11/2: THE INSPIRATIONAL TEACHER

Since 11/2 is a higher octave of number 2, also read the 2 description for greater understanding and insight.

Enlightened 11/2s are the Inspirational Teachers of the world, and their greatest gift is their ability to uplift and inspire others. In their quest to attain a higher level of consciousness and reach their full potential, they pass their teachings on to others—to enable *them* to reach their full potential, too. Master Number 11/2s are the most intuitive of all the numbers, and they combine the individuality, creativity, and leadership of 1 with the sensitivity, intuition, and compassion of 2, to promote peace and raise spiritual awareness on planet Earth. They're also known as the Spiritual Messengers.

Master Number 11/2s are idealistic visionaries who can see the potential in others and the world, but they must attain balance in every area of their lives and distinguish between fantasy and reality in order to achieve their goals. They have imaginative and inventive minds, and the passion, enthusiasm, and charisma to inspire others with their ideas; however, they must follow through with practical action to accomplish their desired results. Confident and proactive 11/2s can attract abundance, success, and even fame when they live by their higher ideals.

Self-understanding is vital to the success of 11/2s, and they must learn to take responsibility for the role they play in the events of their lives. They must be honest with respect to their actions and intentions, and live by their higher ideals rather than manipulate people or the truth to get their own way. Through many tests, trials, and tribulations, they learn about life and accept it in a philosophical manner. They then pass on what they've learned to help others improve the circumstances of *their* lives. Despite their mood swings, intense personalities, and somewhat unrealistic views, 11/2s are extremely understanding and kind, and sensitive to others' needs.

11/2's Strengths

- Inspirational
- Uplifting
- Charismatic
- Creative
- Inventive
- Compassionate
- Intuitive
- Illuminating
- Insightful
- Idealistic

11/2's Weaknesses

- Intense
- Dishonest

- Manipulative
- Obsessive
- Jealous
- Possessive
- Unrealistic
- Self-destructive
- Lazy
- Egotistical

Life Lessons

See the "Life Lessons" sections for number 2 and the Master Numbers.

Astrological Equivalent

Most astrologers believe that the astrological equivalent to number 11/2 is a combination of Sagittarius and Aquarius; however, some feel that it also resonates with Cancer and Leo.

Suitable Career Choices

Public speaker, motivational speaker, teacher, life coach, psychologist, counselor, doctor, inventor, electrician, entertainer, film/TV actor or director, politician, musician, writer, spiritual or religious leader, designer, mediator, healer, massage therapist, clairvoyant, alternative therapist, environmentalist, artist, athlete, public figure. (Also see "Suitable Career Choices" for 2 Life Path Number.)

Compatibility

Master Number 11/2s are said to be most compatible with numbers 2, 3, 4, 6, 7, 9, 11/2, 22/4, and 33/6.

11/2 Life Path Number

As an 11/2 Life Path, you're here to walk the path of the Inspirational Teacher who raises spiritual awareness and understanding on planet Earth. Your goal is to achieve self-mastery and discover your spiritual truth, then pass your findings on to others to help transform *their* lives. You're creative, intelligent, and enthusiastic, but you must rise above your ego so that you may trust and believe in yourself. You love very deeply and have a natural ability to uplift and inspire others; however, like your base number, 2, you need to define your personal limits and boundaries and learn to say no. You must learn how to serve another without losing yourself in the process. Once you step into your full power and surrender to your higher ideals, there is nothing you cannot be, do, or have. As an 11/2 Life Path, you're fulfilling your life purpose when you seek to serve the greater good and make a difference in the world.

11/2 Destiny Number

As an 11/2 Destiny, you're destined to be an Inspirational Teacher who raises spiritual awareness and understanding on planet Earth. Your life's mission is to find your spiritual truth and utilize the laws of the Universe to inspire, heal, and teach. As an 11/2 Destiny, you were born to promote peace, cooperation, and harmony and to teach others via your personal lessons and experiences. You're destined to lead by example and guide others toward their own spiritual awareness. Despite being intuitive, understanding, and sensitive to others' needs, you must overcome your tendency to be controlled by your own obsessions. You've been gifted with the ability to uplift, empower, illuminate, and inspire others to reach their full potential—so put your talents to good use.

11/2 Soul Number

As an 11/2 Soul, you long to be an Inspirational Teacher who raises spiritual awareness and understanding on planet Earth. In your heart of hearts, all your soul wants is to promote peace, co-operation, and harmony, and to help others transform their lives. As an 11/2 Soul, you teach from personal experience and lead by example. Through your own personal transformation, you uplift, empower, and inspire others to reach their full potential, too. Every time you seek to illuminate, improve, heal, or reform, you fulfill your heart's desire.

11/2 Personality Number

As an 11/2 Personality, you may be perceived as a charismatic and enthusiastic visionary who can inspire others with ease. You may come across as broadminded, understanding, and wise beyond your years. Depending on the other numbers in your chart, people may see you as a confident and courageous leader or as an emotional and high-strung follower. Either way, there's no denying that your magnetic personality is attractive and your enthusiasm is contagious. To make the best impression, just relax and be yourself.

11/2 Maturity Number

As an 11/2 Maturity Number, you are being steered toward becoming an Inspirational Teacher who raises spiritual awareness and understanding on planet Earth. Your life's goal is to uplift, empower, and inspire others to transform their lives and reach a higher level of consciousness. As you mature, you'll find yourself becoming concerned with social causes and will be drawn to metaphysical pursuits. An 11/2 Maturity Number also indicates enhanced sensitivity, extrasensory perception, and intuition, along with an increased potential to succeed in your chosen field.

11/2 Birth Day Number (11th and 29th)

As an 11/2 Birth Day, you're gifted with the ability to achieve a depth of understanding beyond your years. You're creative, intelligent, and enthusiastic, but you must overcome your insecurities and believe in yourself. You're a natural counselor and healer, with the ability to uplift and inspire others, and your enhanced intuition and insight enable you to a reach a higher level of perception and awareness. Balance, confidence, and honesty are the keys to your success.

11/2 Current Name Number

An 11/2 Current Name enhances your intuition and extrasensory perception. It also enables you to reach a higher level of consciousness so you can make a difference in the world. This number will help you be an effective leader, healer, speaker, writer, entertainer, counselor, inventor, or musician who seeks to serve the greater good. This is the number of the Inspirational Teacher, who inspires others through his or her own personal transformation and experience.

11/2 Checklist

To determine whether you're fully embracing your "11/2-ness," ask yourself these questions:

- *Do I strive to reach a higher level of consciousness and attain self-mastery?*

- *Do I inspire others to believe in themselves and improve their quality of life?*

- *Am I a leader, visionary, mediator, clairvoyant, healer, inventor, writer, musician, speaker, or counselor?*

- *Do I seek to promote peace, love, and harmony on planet Earth?*

11/2 Example

Internationally renowned speaker and best-selling author Dr. Wayne W. Dyer (5-10-1940) is a classic example of a Master Number 11/2 Life Path (using the reducing-down and adding-down methods, when you reduce the year 1940 to 14), fulfilling his life purpose as an Inspirational Teacher and Spiritual Messenger. Originally a guidance counselor and educator, Wayne leads by example and teaches through personal experience, often sharing his own trials and tribulations to enable others to learn and grow, too. With more than 40 self-help books and two movies, *The Shift* and *My Greatest Teacher,* to his credit, Wayne has raised spiritual awareness on planet Earth and has inspired millions of people to transform their lives. Thanks for being the "Father of Inspiration," Wayne. You're a wonderful example for us all!

11/2 Affirmation

"I uplift, inspire, and empower others and create an exceptional life."

Master Number 22/4: The Master Builder

Since 22/4 is a higher octave of number 4, also read the 4 description for greater understanding and insight.

Enlightened 22/4s are the Master Builders of the world, and their greatest gift is their ability to turn dreams into reality through practical application. In their quest to attain self-mastery and reach a higher level of consciousness, they're driven to build, create, or promote something of benefit to the community or humanity as a whole. Master Number 22/4s are here to create or become involved with a project, organization, product, or service that bridges the material and spiritual worlds. Whether this endeavor takes place on a local or international scale doesn't matter, provided that it seeks to serve the greater good.

Master Number 22/4s are practical planners and dreamers who have the visionary and intuitive insight of 11, the sensitivity and compassion of 2, and the practicality and determination of 4, which is the ultimate combination to turn ideas into physical form. Their ability to see the bigger picture and follow through with practical action enables them to achieve their goals and assist the evolution of humankind. However, despite their enormous potential for success, their overwhelming fear of failure often causes them to abort their hopes and dreams.

Master Number 22/4s must learn to master the hypersensitivity and insecurity of their double 2s to achieve their full potential. They are natural leaders who have the ability to reach great heights within their chosen fields, whether it's in the corporate, scientific, health, technological, political, creative, humanitarian, or metaphysical arena. If they can attain mental, emotional, and physical balance and remain grounded at all time—with discipline, effort, and determination—they can become the Master Builders of humanity.

22/4's Strengths

- Visionary
- Inventive
- Inspirational
- Forward-thinking
- Dedicated
- Focused

99

- Idealistic
- Charismatic
- Creative
- Intuitive

22/4's Weaknesses

- Controlling
- Inflexible
- Workaholic
- Self-destructive
- Awkward
- Arrogant
- Stubborn
- Demanding
- Self-righteous
- Lazy

Life Lessons

See the "Life Lessons" sections for number 4 and the Master Numbers.

Astrological Equivalent

Most astrologers believe that the astrological equivalent to number 22/4 is a combination of Capricorn and Leo; however, some feel that it also resonates with Taurus, Cancer, and Virgo.

Suitable Career Choices

CEO, business owner, manager, politician, diplomat, architect, engineer, inspirational speaker, spiritual leader, government worker or civil servant, social worker, doctor, health or education professional, law-enforcement professional, healer, scientist, inventor, alternative therapist, organization leader. (Also see "Suitable Career Choices" for 4 Life Path Number.)

Compatibility

Master Number 22/4s are said to be most compatible with numbers 1, 2, 4, 6, 7, 8, 9, 11/2, 22/4, and 33/6.

22/4 Life Path Number

As a 22/4 Life Path, you're here to walk the path of the Master Builder who turns dreams into reality through practical application. Your logical and methodical approach makes you a talented organizer and manager of people and projects. When living in the positive, you're a realistic visionary who can see the bigger picture; however, you must remain balanced, grounded, and centered at all times to actualize your dreams. When you have the maturity, self-confidence, and motivation to achieve your goals, the Universe will support you, as long as you seek to serve the greater good.

When you overcome your inferiority complex and trust in others enough to allow them to contribute to your dreams, you have much potential for success. Despite appearing emotionally controlled and contained, you're highly sensitive, intuitive, and caring. As a 22/4 Life Path, you're fulfilling your life purpose when you build, create, or promote something that benefits humanity and bridges the spiritual and material worlds.

22/4 Destiny Number

As a 22/4 Destiny, you're destined to be a Master Builder who turns dreams into reality through practical application. Your life's mission is to help rebuild your community and/or the world on a more solid and secure foundation—one that is grounded in co-operation, peace, and harmony. As a 22/4 Destiny, you're a hard-working visionary, with the ability to bring dreams to fruition with your logical, practical, and methodical approach, provided that you don't let your insecurities get the best of you. So step into your power and put your talents to good use.

22/4 Soul Number

As a 22/4 Soul, you long to be a Master Builder who turns dreams into reality through practical application. In your heart of hearts, all your soul wants is to build, create, or promote some-thing that benefits humanity and bridges the spiritual and mate-rial worlds. As a 22/4 Soul, you're motivated by big projects and challenges that enable you to make a difference in the workplace, community, or world at large. Every time you dream big and see your vision through to completion with your methodical ap-proach, you fulfill your heart's desire.

22/4 Personality Number

As a 22/4 Personality, you may be perceived as somebody with an agenda who follows through with practical action to achieve his or her goals. You come across as hardworking, trustworthy, fo-cused, and committed to your work. People may approach you for practical advice, motivation, and guidance as they seek to attain their own dreams. To make the best impression and avoid being viewed as an uptight workaholic, try to relax and have some fun!

22/4 Maturity Number

As a 22/4 Maturity Number, you are being steered toward becoming a Master Builder who turns dreams into reality through practical application. Your life's goal is to advance the causes that are most pressing to humanity. As you mature, you'll find yourself becoming more interested in community or humanitarian endeavors and taking on management or leadership roles within an organization or project. A 22/4 Maturity Number also indicates the potential for major accomplishments in areas that serve the greater good.

22/4 Birth Day Number

As a 22/4 Birth Day, you're gifted with the ability to govern or build something for the benefit of others. You're a hardworking visionary, with the ability to bring your dreams to fruition, but you must learn to master the hypersensitivity and insecurity of your double 2s in the process. Your logical, practical, and methodical approach makes you a talented organizer and manager; however, another life lesson is to remain balanced, grounded, and steadfast in the face of adversity and hardship.

22/4 Current Name Number

A 22/4 Current Name enhances your ability to overcome obstacles and achieve your goals. It also enables you to dream on a larger scale and influence others to contribute to the manifestation of your dreams. This number will help you become a hardworking visionary, with the potential to build, create, govern, or promote something for the benefit of humankind.

22/4 Checklist

To determine whether you're fully embracing your "22/4-ness," ask yourself these questions:

- *Am I building, creating, or promoting something that will have a positive impact on the community and/or the world?*

- *Am I a leader who motivates and inspires others with my vision of a better world?*

- *Am I a hardworking visionary who dreams big and follows through with practical action?*

- *Am I driven to promote cooperation, peace, and harmony on planet Earth?*

22/4 Example

International speaker, author, and Nobel Peace Prize winner His Holiness the 14th Dalai Lama (7-6-1935) is a classic example of a Master Number 22/4 Life Path (using the reducing-down and adding-down methods), fulfilling his life purpose as a Master Builder promoting something for the benefit of humankind—world peace! He travels the globe teaching Tibetan Buddhism and speaking on a variety of topics, such as economics, the environment, and equal rights. He also lectures about the importance of meditation, compassion, and happiness to improve one's quality of life. Thank you, Your Holiness. We appreciate your wisdom and applaud your efforts!

22/4 Affirmation

*"I build something for the benefit of humanity
and improve my own life in turn."*

Master Number 33/6: The Cosmic Parent

Since 33/6 is a higher octave of number 6, also read the 6 description for greater understanding and insight.

Enlightened 33/6s are the Cosmic Parents of the world who raise the vibration of humanity through their service, creativity, and compassion. Even though evolved 33/6s are extremely rare finds, they have the ability to heal the masses with their unconditional love. Whether they bring joy and happiness into the world through a career in service, teaching, healing, or the arts, they're the champions of the underdog who feel a deep responsibility toward others. Master Number 33/6s are also known as the *Masters of Healing Energies.*

Due to the perfectionism of the 6 combined with a double dose of sensitivity and insecurity from the double 3s, many 33/6s are emotional high achievers who crave approval from others and can never quite meet their own idealistic standards. However, once they accept and fully embrace their imperfection and that of others and the world, they can reach their full potential and actualize their dreams. Like their base number, 6, 33/6s are natural parents and caregivers who are here to learn about responsibility and self-sacrifice. Like all 6s, they're also here to master lessons in love. Due to the presence of the double 3s, they must use positive avenues to express themselves—such as a creative hobby or the literary, visual, or performing arts—rather than the negative forms of expression 3s sometimes fall prey to such as gossiping, criticizing, or complaining.

Even though at the present time very few people in the world have reached the level of self-mastery required to live up to the Master Number 33/6 vibration, 33/6s are still the master teachers and healers of the world whose life purpose is to evolve through loving service to others. During the course of their lives, they'll witness the suffering of others, and be aware of many injustices in the world. As a result, they must learn to detach from their personal feelings in order to effect significant positive change.

33/6's Strengths

- Creative
- Joyful
- Compassionate
- Intuitive
- Inspirational
- Uplifting
- Healing
- Loving
- Family oriented
- Nurturing

33/6's Weaknesses

- Perfectionistic
- Critical
- Self-righteous
- People-pleasing
- Judgmental
- Intolerant
- Bossy
- Self-critical
- Interfering
- Overachieving

Life Lessons

See the "Life Lessons" sections for number 6 and the Master Numbers.

Astrological Equivalent

Most astrologers believe that the astrological equivalent to number 33/6 is a combination of Libra, Sagittarius, and Pisces; however, some feel that it also resonates with Cancer and Leo.

Suitable Career Choices

Entertainer; actor; musician; healer; spiritual teacher; dancer; artist; environmentalist; clairvoyant; public speaker; motivational speaker; hairstylist; designer; decorator; counselor; therapist; doctor or other health professional; chef; caregiver; alternative therapist; child-care professional; schoolteacher; stay-at-home mom or dad; homemaker; color consultant; literary, visual, or performing artist. (Also see "Suitable Career Choices" for 6 Life Path Number.)

Compatibility

Master Number 33/6s are said to be most compatible with numbers 2, 3, 4, 6, 8, 9, 11/2, 22/4, and 33/6.

33/6 Life Path Number

As a 33/6 Life Path, you're here to walk the path of the Cosmic Parent who brings joy and happiness into the world through your creativity and compassion. You're an extremely talented caregiver, with a natural tendency to heal; however, one of your life lessons is to learn not to interfere with others' free will in the quest to heal their lives. You're helpful and sympathetic and have a gift for working with children. Due to the fun-loving energy of your double 3s, you're a child at heart yourself. Your creativity, sensitivity, and compassion are much-needed gifts in the world. When you maintain emotional and spiritual balance, you can achieve greatness. As a 33/6 Life Path, you're fulfilling your life purpose when you dedicate yourself to being of service through teaching, healing, or creative expression.

33/6 Destiny Number

As a 33/6 Destiny, you're destined to be a Cosmic Parent who brings joy and happiness into the world through your creativity and compassion. Your life's mission is to promote unconditional love and joy and to heal the pain of the world. You're destined to raise the love vibration of the planet to its highest possible level and to help humanity reach its highest understanding of love through joyful service. As a 33/6 Destiny, you're a talented teacher, healer, parent, communicator, artist, and entertainer . . . so put your talents to good use.

33/6 Soul Number

As a 33/6 Soul, you long to be a Cosmic Parent who brings joy and happiness into the world through your creativity and compassion. In your heart of hearts, all your soul wants is to raise the vibration on planet Earth and to heal through unconditional love. It strives to attain self-mastery through loving service to others. As a 33/6 Soul, you're motivated by being of service to those in need and by teaching others about happiness and love. Every time you are involved in teaching, healing, or expressing yourself creatively, you fulfill your heart's desire.

33/6 Personality Number

As a 33/6 Personality, you may be perceived as a natural counselor who is ready, willing, and able to lend a helping hand. Even though you are kindhearted, sympathetic, and compassionate, you may also be viewed as an idealistic overachiever who's overly concerned with doing the right thing or being viewed in the best possible light. People may see you as someone who puts family first and is concerned with the well-being of others. To make the best impression, try to be less critical of yourself and others and more accepting of people's shortcomings.

33/6 Maturity Number

As a 33/6 Maturity Number, you are being steered toward becoming a Cosmic Parent who brings joy and happiness into the world through your creativity and compassion. You may find yourself becoming a teacher, healer, counselor, artist, or entertainer. Your life's goal is to attain self-mastery through loving service to others and by healing through unconditional love. As you mature, you'll find yourself becoming more concerned with the welfare of others and will be drawn to humanitarian pursuits. As you begin to acutely feel the pain of the world, you may be driven to make a difference in some way. A 33/6 Maturity Number also indicates an element of self-sacrifice and responsibility toward humankind.

33/6 Current Name Number

A 33/6 Current Name enhances your ability to counsel, teach, inspire, and heal others. It also enables you to dedicate your life to being in service, if you so choose. This number will help you work more effectively with children and be a better parent, caregiver, and communicator. It will enhance your creative talents and abilities and allow you to be more sympathetic and compassionate toward others.

33/6 Checklist

To determine whether you're fully embracing your "33/6-ness," ask yourself these questions:

- *Am I a healer, teacher, entertainer, artist, or leader in the metaphysical arena?*

- *Do I heal, motivate, or inspire others with my creativity and vision of a better world?*

- *Do I use laughter and the arts to bring joy to the world?*

- *Do I wish to be—or am I already—teaching, parenting, or working with children?*

33/6 Example

To find a 33/6 Life Path using both the reducing-down and adding-across methods is very rare; however, award-winning actress Meryl Streep (6-22-1949) is a classic example of a genuine 33/6. Her Master Number 33/6 Life Path and 22/4 Birth Day enable her to fulfill her life purpose as a Cosmic Parent and Master Builder who brings happiness and healing into the world through her creative pursuits. Meryl has secretly donated millions of dollars to charities and schools over the years, and continues to support a wide variety of causes. (Oxfam, Artists for Peace and Justice, Equity Fights AIDS, Healthy Child–Healthy World, Equality Now, and Stand Up to Cancer are some of the charities and foundations she has supported over the years.) Thank you for your love, kindness, and generosity, Meryl . . . and for bringing joy into the world through your flawless creative expression!

33/6 Affirmation

"I fulfill my life purpose to love, teach, and heal humanity."

�֍

Now let's take a look at the meanings of the Karmic Debt Numbers for added information and insight.

110

KARMIC DEBT NUMBERS

If you have a 13/4, 14/5, 16/7, or 19/1 in your 7 Core Numbers, it's considered a Karmic Debt Number. Karmic Debt Numbers indicate particular lessons that failed to be learned in previous lives and which must be mastered in *this* lifetime. They can also indicate the abuse of a particular gift or position of power in a previous life. Each Karmic Debt Number has its own unique lessons and burdens. (Karmic Debt Numbers are not to be confused with Karmic Lesson Numbers, covered in the previous chapter.)

KARMIC DEBT NUMBER 13/4

This number indicates that extra effort is required to accomplish your desired goals due to a need to master discipline, integrity, and determination in this life. With a 13/4 among your Core Numbers, you must learn to be responsible and face your challenges head-on rather than succumb to quick-fix solutions, shortcuts, or manipulation. Karmic Debt Number 13/4 brings an opportunity for personal transformation, and when you're honest, patient, and persevere through adversity, you'll overcome this lesson.

KARMIC DEBT NUMBER 14/5

This number indicates a need to display temperance and moderation in every area of your life and to be mindful of overindulgence. With a 14/5 among your Core Numbers, you must learn to rise above temptation and earthly desires in favor of responsibility and honoring your commitments. By balancing your desire for freedom and adventure with your responsibilities, you'll overcome this lesson.

KARMIC DEBT NUMBER 16/7

This number indicates a need to reevaluate your core values and eliminate any superficial foundations that do not align with your higher self. With a 16/7 among your Core Numbers, you must

111

learn to rise above your ego and pride, treat others with respect, trust and surrender to the unexpected events in your life, and be honest and faithful in love. When you focus on your personal development and rise above your superficial tendencies, you'll overcome this lesson.

Karmic Debt Number 19/1

This number indicates a sense of frustration due to your inability to control everything and everyone in your life. With a 19/1 among your Core Numbers, you must learn to take others' needs, feelings, and opinions into consideration rather than just your own. By having the courage to accept assistance from others, admit your mistakes, and see differing points of view (regardless of whether they're right or wrong), you'll overcome this lesson.

✦ ✦ ✦

Understanding Your Numerology Profile

As a human being, you have free will to decide whether or not to follow the prechosen numerological blueprint of your life; however, the more in tune you are with your inner calling, the truer you will be to your numbers. Upon reading the characteristics of your numbers, you may come across particular traits, talents, or abilities you didn't realize you had. It isn't uncommon for these characteristics to present themselves in the years to come once you've learned to overcome the challenges that prevent you from being your true, authentic self. On the other hand, you'd be surprised to learn how often these traits, talents, and abilities are visibly present, yet you yourself fail to see them. Therefore, it pays to ask someone who knows you well, such as a family member, partner, or friend, for his or her opinion. Oftentimes, this person will confirm that those characteristics exist in you.

When evaluating your numerology profile (and the numerology profiles of others), remember to take your outside influences into consideration for greater accuracy. Outside influences such as your parents, upbringing, childhood experiences, extended family, peer group, community, cultural background, and religious and political beliefs can have a significant effect on the expression of your numbers. For example, a 3 Life Path may not follow a dream of being an artist where there is family pressure to become a lawyer; or a 1 Life Path may not be as outgoing and courageous if he or she was, or currently is, the victim of abuse.

With that being said, regardless of one's life circumstances and outside influences, the numbers will automatically provide the necessary traits, strengths, and abilities to overcome adversity so that anyone can attain his or her best and highest self. The more you think for yourself; love and respect who you are; listen to your intuition; follow your inner guidance; and attend to your own needs with meditation, exercise, a healthy diet, conscious breathing, prayer, and positive thinking, the easier it will be to reach your full numerological potential as your true, authentic self.

PART II

Forecasting
and Timing

Your Cycle Numbers

Like the seasons in a year, your life journey is divided into seasons as well. In fact, your life is an ongoing pattern of cycles designed for your personal growth. A numerology cycle can predict your environment and destination; it can even forecast the conditions under which you're traveling on your journey. But due to your free will to think and behave as you choose, it cannot anticipate the decisions you'll make or the actions you'll take on your path.

That being said, it certainly helps to know where you're going and the conditions under which you're traveling at any given time. For example, if you decided to take a road trip to an unfamiliar destination, wouldn't you prefer to consult a map to see where you're going and check the driving conditions before you hit the road? Well, you can think of your numerology cycles as the "road maps" of your life.

Your name and date of birth reveal your destiny, along with a step-by-step process that will help you fulfill it to the best of your abilities. Your *cycles* reveal the intricate details of that process, and when you surrender to its guidance rather than push against the natural flow, you'll reach your full potential and improve your quality of life. Once you understand and surrender to the natural rhythm of your cycles, life becomes a heck of a lot easier! Now, you may not be able to avoid life's challenges altogether, but when you know that there's trouble ahead, you can be better equipped and prepared.

VARIOUS CYCLES, REPETITIVE MEANINGS

In numerology, there are several interacting cycles that vary in length. Some are long-term cycles ranging between 25 and 35 years, while others are of a shorter duration such as one month or one year. At first it can seem pretty overwhelming to try to remember them all and what they represent, but to make things a little easier, remember the following: *A number has the same meaning wherever it appears.* Once you have the number meanings down pat, forecasting the future is as easy as painting by numbers!

Because *a number has the same meaning wherever it appears,* I suggest you read *all* of the cycle-number descriptions for a particular number for additional insight as to what that Cycle Number represents. In other words, to learn more about your 8 Major Life Cycle Number, read the 8 Pinnacle, 8 Personal Year, and 8 Essence Number descriptions for a deeper understanding of what's to come.

✳

Now let's begin with the Major Life Cycles.

MAJOR LIFE CYCLES

The *Major Life Cycles*—otherwise known as the *Growth Cycles, Cycles of Growth, Life Cycles, Period Cycles, Major Cycles, Cycles of Life,* or *Life Path Periods*—divide your Life Path Number journey into three blocks of time that highlight the three stages of growth throughout your life. These three blocks of time are often called the *Formative, Productive,* and *Harvest Years,* and many refer to the stages of growth as the *Cycles of Youth, Maturity,* and *Wisdom.* You can think of your Major Life Cycles as the three areas of development that will help you fulfill your destiny as you journey along your life path.

Each Major Life Cycle Number has its own unique theme, and the length of each cycle varies between 25 and 35 years depending on which system you use. Sometimes the transitional shift between each cycle can be strongly felt, and other times it can go unnoticed. It all depends on the cycle numbers involved and the other numbers in your chart. It also depends on your mind-set and life circumstances at the time of transition.

You may not feel the influence of your Major Life Cycles as strongly as some of the other cycles in your chart, such as the Personal Year, Personal Month, Pinnacles, Challenges, and Essence Number cycles (which we'll discuss a bit further on); however, they uncover the story of your life. When you understand your Major Life Cycles and what they represent, you can take advantage of the opportunities to come and prepare yourself for the changes ahead. And when you harmonize with the natural flow of your numbers, you can minimize stress and increase synchronicity in your life. Now that sounds pretty good, doesn't it?

How to Calculate Your Major Life Cycle Numbers

There are three Major Life Cycle Numbers that are calculated from the numbers in your birth date. First, begin by reducing the month, day, and year numbers of your birth date down to three single-digit numbers unless they total 11 or 22. If you have an 11 or 22 month, day, or year—that is, if you were born in November (11); on the 11th, 22nd, or 29th of your birth month; or in a year that totals 11 or 22, such as 1975 ($1 + 9 + 7 + 5 = 22$)—it doesn't reduce down to 2 or 4 but rather remains 11 or 22.

Let's use the birth date December 11, 1969 (12-11-1969), as an example:

12 / 11/ 1969
$\underline{1+2}$ / $\underline{11}$ / $\underline{1+9+6+9}$ = 25
  3   **11** $\underline{2+5}$
                        7

Therefore, the three single digits for birth date 12-11-1969 are 3, 11, and 7.

First Major Life Cycle Number

This is the number of your birth month.

Depending on your Life Path Number and which Major Life Cycle period calculation method you use, this cycle influences the first 25 to 35 years of your life. It's called the *Cycle of Youth* and governs your Formative years. This is a period of learning and self-discovery.

In our example birth date, December 11, 1969, the First Major Life Cycle Number is 3.

Second Major Life Cycle Number

This is the number of your birth day.

Depending on which Major Life Cycle period calculation method you use, this cycle influences the next 27 to 28 years of your life. It's called the *Cycle of Maturity* and governs your Productive years. This is a period of stabilization and finding your place in the world. This is where you work hard to implement your ideas and achieve your goals.

In our example birth date, December 11, 1969, the Second Major Life Cycle Number is 11.

Third Major Life Cycle Number

This is the number of your birth year.

This cycle influences the remaining years of your life. It's called the *Cycle of Wisdom* and governs your Harvest years. This is a period of self-empowerment and specialization, where your accumulated wisdom and experience enables you to reach your full potential.

In our example birth date, December 11, 1969, the Third Major Life Cycle Number is 7.

(It's possible to repeat the same Major Life Cycle Number in a chart.)

How to Calculate Your Major Life Cycle Periods

A conflicting point among numerologists is the designation of the Major Life Cycle periods. Some use a straightforward 28-year cycle to calculate each of the three periods, making the first cycle period birth to 28 years, the second 29 to 56 years, and the third from 57 years onward; whereas others simply add 28 to the Life Path Number and go from there. Then there are those who believe the First Major Life Cycle period is from birth until the age of transition from the First to Second Pinnacle Number (as discussed in the "Pinnacles" segment to follow). Numerologists who follow this particular method calculate the Major Life Cycle periods as follows:

First Major Life Cycle Period

From birth until the age of transition from the First to the Second Pinnacle Number.

Second Major Life Cycle Period

Twenty-seven years from the end of the First Major Life Cycle period.

Third Major Life Cycle Period

From the end of the Second Major Life Cycle period until the time of passing.

Other numerologists use Major Life Cycle periods that are based upon the Life Path Number, as shown in the following chart:

Life Path Number	First Cycle	Second Cycle	Third Cycle
1	0–26	27–53	54+
2 and 11	0–25	26–52	53+
3	0–33	34–60	61+
4 and 22	0–32	33–59	60+
5	0–31	32–58	59+
6	0–30	31–57	58+
7	0–29	30–56	57+
8	0–28	29–55	56+
9	0–27	28–54	55+

Once again, the method you decide to use is simply a matter of personal preference.

Please note: *The influence of a new Major Life Cycle Number can be felt up to two years prior to the official change-over period.*

Now let's take a look at the Major Life Cycle Number meanings.

Major Life Cycle Number Meanings

1 Major Life Cycle

Independence, Courage, Individuality, Leadership

As Your First Cycle

Although you may feel like a square peg in a round hole at times, life is teaching you to embrace your individuality and use it to your advantage rather than as an excuse to alienate yourself. Your originality is your point of difference, and it will take you far once you've found your niche and feel confident within yourself. During this cycle, life is encouraging you to be independent, self-sufficient, and self-motivated so you can make your mark on the world. You'll learn to stand up for yourself and your beliefs— in some instances, in preparation for leadership.

As Your Second Cycle

Your entrepreneurial and leadership abilities will come to the forefront during this cycle, if they haven't done so already. You'll find yourself stepping up to the plate and taking charge of your life like never before. This is a cycle of self-motivation and empowerment, with many opportunities for achievement. Life is encouraging you to become an innovative self-starter within your personal life and career. It's during this cycle that you'll discover that there's nothing you cannot be, do, or have when you utilize your talents and have unwavering self-confidence and faith.

As Your Third Cycle

During this cycle, you're given an opportunity to reinvent yourself or to rise to a position of authority. Now that you've reached the necessary level of maturity to become an effective leader, the Universe will send you plenty of opportunities to lead. To have a 1 Cycle of Wisdom during your Harvest years is a very powerful omen. Now that you have the courage to be yourself and are no longer influenced by others' opinions, you can stand in your full power and actualize your dreams.

2 Major Life Cycle

Sensitivity, Intuition, Cooperation, Balance

As Your First Cycle

This can be a highly sensitive period as you strive to develop your self-confidence and balance your emotions. You have the potential to excel in creative and musical endeavors and will learn to be part of a team. Partnership and emotional connection to others come to the forefront as you discover what it means to love and be loved, and possibly to have loved and lost. You'll find yourself playing a supportive or counseling role to family, partners, and friends. It's during this cycle that you'll learn how to cooperate with others and resolve conflicts harmoniously.

As Your Second Cycle

During this cycle, you'll realize the importance of a harmonious environment and maintaining emotional balance. In fact, *balance* is the main focus of this cycle. Finding balance in every area of your life—whether it's between giving and receiving, between intuition and logic, or simply between your home life and your career—is the key to your success. Love, relationships, and family are your number one priorities during this cycle. Your counseling, healing, nurturing, and negotiation skills develop during this cycle.

As Your Third Cycle

A 2 Cycle of Wisdom during your Harvest years enables you to love, nurture, and heal from a place of balance and power. You're the backbone of the family and play a major role in creating peace among your loved ones, friends, and possibly the community.

People seek you out for your kindness, assistance, understanding, and wisdom, and your musical, creative, and healing abilities are at an all-time high. There is much love, friendship, and companionship in your later years.

3 Major Life Cycle

Creativity, Self-Expression, Social Activity, Joy

As Your First Cycle

This is the ideal first cycle for a young person, because it focuses on fun, friendship, and creative expression. This cycle is all about finding your voice and learning to speak your truth, and music, writing, body movement, and art enable you to express yourself with greater ease. This can be a highly sensitive time as you learn to identify your feelings and put them into words. Communication is the key to improving your quality of life. Self-discipline is essential during this cycle to avoid a "play now, pay later" mentality or becoming a jack-of-all-trades and master of none. With focus and dedication, this can be a very rewarding cycle.

As Your Second Cycle

During this cycle, there's an opportunity to develop any creative talent that you may have and possibly even turn it into a career, especially if you have a 2, 3, 6, 9, 11/2, or 33/6 among your Core Numbers. At the very least, you'll have a strong desire to express yourself creatively—whether it be verbally, intellectually, conceptually, or artistically. It doesn't really matter what you do, because any form of creative expression is favored during this time. You'll find that you have the gift of gab and the charisma to attract supporters—but focus, discipline, and confidence are keys to your success. This is a time of family, fun, and friendship where you learn to identify your emotions, be optimistic, and speak your truth.

As Your Third Cycle

A 3 Cycle of Wisdom during your Harvest years promises social activity, friendship, and fun. This is one of the most favorable cycles to retire under, provided that you have a positive mindset about life. You'll find plenty of people, activities, and hobbies to help keep you entertained, and you're bound to tap into your creative side to explore artistic and/or intellectual pursuits. Humor, good conversation, and laughter play a major role during this cycle. Despite the typical ups and downs people tend to experience during their later years, as long as you're fit and healthy, you'll be more carefree and relaxed than you've ever been before. Downsize the drama in your life to make it a favorable cycle.

4 Major Life Cycle

Building, Planning, Effort, Discipline, Focus

As Your First Cycle

This cycle during your Formative years will teach you about the importance of physical, financial, and emotional stability. During this cycle, you'll learn that results can only be obtained from building a secure and stable foundation. This is where you'll learn the value of integrity, honesty, discipline, and hard work. You'll discover that with patience and perseverance, you can make your dreams come true. Although you may feel held back or restricted in some way, with good old-fashioned values and morals, there is much potential for success.

As Your Second Cycle

This is a cycle where, with hard work and effort, you can set yourself up for life. Routine, organization, sound decision making, and financial discipline will enable you to get ahead—provided that you take your responsibilities seriously and commit to your goals. You'll become the backbone of your family and possibly your workplace, the community, or an organization during this cycle; however, you'll need to balance your home life with your career and set aside time for relaxation and fun. Much is expected from you during this time, and you'll have your fair share of challenges, but if you persist, you'll be rewarded for your efforts.

As Your Third Cycle

A 4 Cycle of Wisdom during your Harvest years provides security and stability through careful planning, sound decision making, and financial discipline. Typically this isn't a cycle where you'll want to retire and twiddle your thumbs. If you're physically fit and able, you'll wish to keep yourself stimulated and busy by working on a project, hobby, or job. You have a gift for organizing and managing others and remain the backbone of your family, workplace, or community until you're no longer able. You'll want to keep earning money to provide a legacy of financial security to those you leave behind.

5 Major Life Cycle

Exploration, Experience, Freedom, Communication

As Your First Cycle

A 5 cycle during your Formative years brings about activity, movement, and change. If you're stimulated by variety and action, this can be a very exciting time; however, if you crave stability and routine, it can prove to be a challenge. Either way, you'll meet many fascinating people and develop a variety of interests. As you come of age, you may begin to push conventional boundaries and experiment with alcohol, sex, or anything else that stimulates your senses. Since 5 is a scattered energy, extra effort is required to create stability in your personal life and career.

As Your Second Cycle

Because 5 is the number of freedom and adventure, you may, depending on the other numbers in your chart, find this to be a challenging cycle to settle down under. On the other hand, you may find that it's the perfect time to raise a family and commit to domestic life experiences. If you already have a 5 among your Core Numbers, domestic responsibilities and constraints may cause you to feel trapped at times; therefore, relationships that allow you to enjoy personal freedom have the greatest chance of success. During this cycle, you may travel, change your career, and move to another home or city. You'll meet many interesting people and experience many different things. Your ability to teach and communicate effectively with others is greatly enhanced.

As Your Third Cycle

This is a stimulating and adventurous cycle to be in during your Harvest years. If you're physically and financially able to travel, there will be many opportunities to do so. Age doesn't seem to be an issue during this time, as you'll crave an active retirement and have the energy to back it up. You'll meet a variety of interesting people and will continue to learn new things. This is an action-packed cycle, with plenty of things to see and do, so plan, focus, and prioritize. Now you're finally free to do whatever you want with your time!

6 Major Life Cycle

Love, Family, Domestic Responsibility, Creativity

As Your First Cycle

During this cycle, you'll learn about family dynamics and values, and the importance of playing your part within the group. There may be an element of self-sacrifice as you fulfill your obligation to be of service to your family. You'll try to be a good person and do the right thing; however, during this time you'll discover that the perfect person doesn't exist. You could marry early or become a parent during this cycle, especially if you have a 6 among your Core Numbers. Love and relationships come to the forefront regardless of your age.

As Your Second Cycle

This is a favorable cycle in which to get married, start a family, and fulfill your domestic responsibilities; on the other hand, there is also potential for an unstable relationship or marriage to come to an end. You're the pillar of your family during this cycle and will learn to put others' needs before your own; however, you must define your personal boundaries and find the balance between giving and receiving. There will be opportunities to advance in your career, but you'll need to balance your work obligations with your home responsibilities. Your creative ability is greatly enhanced during this cycle, as is your ability to love and be loved. Love and relationships take center stage at this time.

As Your Third Cycle

A 6 Cycle of Wisdom brings about the opportunity to create a content and happy home. During this cycle, you're the rock of your family and circle of friends. You become the shoulder to cry on and the one everyone seeks out for advice. Your desire to nurture, teach, and serve may even extend to your grandchildren and the community at large. Either way, you have a gift for helping, teaching, and healing, and you put those talents to good use. Your creative abilities are enhanced during this cycle, as is your flair for beautifying the home. You may be drawn to gardening, cooking, and decorating more than ever before. This cycle promises loving relationships and meaningful connections with friends in which you'll be called upon to assist those in need.

7 Major Life Cycle

Introspection, Specialization, Spirituality, Personal Growth

As Your First Cycle

This cycle focuses on your inner development as you obtain a deeper understanding of life from a very early age. Whether you are raised in a religious household or have the freedom to discover your own spiritual beliefs, you'll find yourself in a position where you question the meaning of life. You may enjoy spending time on your own and may feel different in some way; that said, this is the ultimate cycle during which to study and become a specialist in your chosen pursuit.

As Your Second Cycle

During this cycle, you may be drawn to metaphysics, alternative or conventional health, technology, science, psychology, philosophy, or other academic subjects. With dedication and focus, you can become a master at your craft. You have a natural ability to learn, analyze, and retain information and pass it on to others; therefore, you may also be drawn to teaching, researching, reporting, or communicating your wisdom and truth. Quiet time by yourself is essential to your well-being, and you may find yourself defending your need to be alone. This is a time of major personal growth where you ponder the meaning of life. Meditation, faith, prayer, and spirituality are the keys to your success.

<u>As Your Third Cycle</u>

Under the influence of a 7 Cycle of Wisdom, you'll crave quiet time alone to focus on your personal and spiritual growth; therefore, it pays to have an understanding partner and family members who support you in your quest. You'll benefit greatly from prayer, meditation, conscious breathing techniques, and energy-related modalities such as yoga and qigong. Your intuition is greatly enhanced, as is your ability to understand universal laws. You'll wish to uncover the secrets and mysteries of the Universe and may explore metaphysics, alternative or conventional health, technology, science, philosophy, psychology, or other academic pursuits. As you grow in understanding and wisdom, you'll be given many opportunities to teach what you have learned.

8 Major Life Cycle

Personal Power, Manifestation, Finances, Career

<u>As Your First Cycle</u>

During this cycle, you'll learn to appreciate the value of money and the importance of financial stability. Whether you're raised in poverty or within a wealthy or materialistic home, you'll learn from personal experience that optimism, effort, and financial discipline will help you get ahead in life. Under the influence of an 8 Formative Cycle, you could go into business at an early age. You could become a leader or supervisor of others or an entrepreneurial self-starter. Either way, this cycle will teach you about morals, money, power, and the secrets of success. You may find yourself having to reclaim your personal power by confronting a person, mind-set, or behavior that has taken that power away.

As Your Second Cycle

This is a fortunate cycle if you have a good work ethic and solid values and morals, and you wish to rise to a position of authority and advance in your career. Whether you're self-employed or work for another, there will be opportunities to improve your finances and gain recognition for your work. Honesty and integrity are vital during this cycle, as 8 represents the Law of Cause and Effect. In some cases, but not all, 8 can also indicate a reversal of fortune and a need to rebuild your foundation. Provided that you have a healthy relationship with money, adopt an attitude of abundance, and keep your ego in check, you can easily attain your goals and set yourself up for life. During this cycle, you'll learn not to let money, status, and power define you.

As Your Third Cycle

With an 8 Major Life Cycle during your Harvest years, you won't want to retire and just kick back. You're a gifted manager and leader with a knack for recognizing talent in others. Whether you're the CEO of a corporation or the president of your tennis club, you'll continue to utilize your skills until you're no longer able. With sound decision making and financial discipline, you can acquire a nice little nest egg for your future. If you haven't yet learned the importance of financial discipline and security, you will during this cycle. Whether you've worked hard and saved for your retirement, you've received an inheritance or payoff from a successful business venture, or the scales of justice have tilted in your favor, with an attitude of abundance, you can retire financially secure.

9 Major Life Cycle

Compassion, Humanitarianism, Service, Creativity

As Your First Cycle

A 9 cycle during your Formative years will teach you broad-mindedness and compassion. You'll be faced with many situations that will encourage you to see the bigger picture so you can understand human behavior. This can be a challenging cycle at times as you struggle to develop tolerance, compassion, and forgiveness with limited life experience and understanding. Upon the conclusion of this cycle, you'll either be drawn to helping others or be more focused on helping yourself. Your creative abilities are enhanced during this cycle, and you may find yourself drawn to the literary, performing, or visual arts.

As Your Second Cycle

This cycle focuses on forgiveness, patience, compassion, and tolerance toward others and yourself. You'll be exposed to many different cultures and ways of life to broaden your horizons. This is a time of greater social awareness where you may be drawn to a cause that serves the community, humanity, animals, or the environment. This is a powerful cycle of personal transformation that will change your entire life. As with all 9 cycles, your creative abilities are enhanced, and you are encouraged to participate in the literary, performing, or visual arts.

As Your Third Cycle

Provided that you've forgiven others, yourself, and your past, these will be some of the most satisfying years of your life. The wiser you become, the greater your need to pass your wisdom on to others. Whether it's your friends, family, the community, or humanity in general, you feel a need to serve a bigger cause. During this cycle, you may focus on selfless service by donating your time, knowledge, or money without expecting anything in return. You've done a lot of work on yourself over the years and would like to help others do the same. This is a time of self-appreciation and reflection and giving back to the world. It's also a time to follow your creative passions and utilizing your artistic gifts. An interest in the literary, performing, or visual arts is encouraged.

11/2 Major Life Cycle Number

Inspiration, Illumination, Transformation, Spiritual Awakening

Also read the description for 2 Major Life Cycle Number.

As Your First Cycle

During an 11/2 First Major Life Cycle, you're also under the influence of a 2 vibration and will experience everything that falls under it, along with added sensitivity and intuition. You may be gifted in some way or battle insecurity or nerve-related issues. Nevertheless, you have a natural ability to inspire others and excel in psychological, metaphysical, or healing pursuits. Upon the conclusion of this cycle, you will have taken a major leap forward in your personal and spiritual growth.

As Your Second Cycle

During an 11/2 Second Major Life Cycle, you're also under the influence of a 2 vibration and will experience everything that falls under it, along with the potential to excel in counseling, teaching, healing, coaching, public speaking, psychology, or metaphysical pursuits. Whether you choose to take this up as a hobby or as a career, there's much potential for success when you seek to serve the greater good. You have a natural gift for motivating and inspiring others, and this cycle will help you reach the masses if you choose to take that path—provided that you do the work and meet the Universe halfway. You'll experience a deep personal transformation during this cycle and will grow in self-understanding and spiritual awareness.

As Your Third Cycle

During an 11/2 Third Major Life Cycle, you're also under the influence of a 2 vibration and will experience everything that falls under it, along with added confidence, wisdom, and maturity to attain self-mastery. If you're up for the challenge, you may become a messenger who raises spiritual awareness in the community or world. At the very least, you'll be an Inspirational Teacher, motivating others to transform their lives. If you prefer to focus on yourself, you may reach higher levels of understanding and awareness through self-reflection and study. Either way, this is a cycle of deep personal transformation where you can become an effective leader of others once you find harmony within yourself.

22/4 Major Life Cycle Number

Commitment, Achievement, Establishment, Spiritual Awakening

Also read the description for 4 Major Life Cycle Number.

As Your First Cycle

There is no 22/4 First Major Life Cycle, as there is no 22 month.

As Your Second Cycle

During a 22/4 Second Major Life Cycle, you're also under the influence of a 4 vibration and will experience everything that falls under it, along with an added opportunity to do something of benefit for the community or humanity as a whole. During this cycle of spiritual awakening, you may create or be involved with a project, organization, product, or service that bridges the material and spiritual worlds. For example, you may create or promote a service to mainstream society that combines alternative and conventional medicine. Whether this endeavor takes place on a local or international scale doesn't matter, as every little effort counts when it comes to raising the vibration of the whole.

As Your Third Cycle

During a 22/4 Third Major Life Cycle, you're also under the influence of a 4 vibration and will experience everything that falls under it, along with the added potential to achieve greatness when you seek to serve the community or humanity as a whole. If you choose to rise to the challenge, you'll find yourself in a position to bridge the material and spiritual worlds by practical means. During this cycle of spiritual awakening, you may create or be involved with a project, organization, product, or service that bridges the material and spiritual worlds. For example, you may create or promote a product that improves the education system in your country or regional school district. There is the potential for local and international recognition, provided that your intentions are pure. This is a powerful cycle of achievement, because you now have the confidence, wisdom, and maturity to succeed.

PINNACLES

Falling directly under the Major Life Cycles are the four *Pinnacles,* sometimes referred to as the *Peak Numbers.* The Pinnacles reveal the atmosphere and events you'll be faced with during each Pinnacle period, along with your potential areas for achievement. You can think of the Major Life Cycles as the "grand themes" of your life, and the Pinnacles as the "mini-themes" or areas of specialization that can assist you during your Major Life Cycles. When you utilize the opportunities your Pinnacles present, you can increase your potential for success.

Of the four Pinnacle periods, the first and last are of the longest duration, while the middle two are nine years each. The Pinnacles and Challenges (which we'll cover next) work very closely with the Major Life Cycles. In fact, each Major Life Cycle has at least one accompanying Pinnacle and Challenge.

Typically, the transition from one Pinnacle to the next is noticeably stronger than a Major Life Cycle transition. It's not uncommon for a major life experience or event to accompany a Pinnacle change, and it can even take place up to two years in advance of the actual transition. How strongly a Pinnacle transition is felt depends on the Pinnacle Numbers involved, along with your mind-set and life circumstances at the time of transition. The other numbers in your chart play a significant role as well.

Pinnacles are gateways that lead you toward your greatest potential for success. When you work in harmony with your Pinnacles and surrender to the natural flow of events, you'll reach your highest potential with greater efficiency and ease.

How to Calculate Your Pinnacle Numbers

There are four Pinnacle Numbers that are calculated from the numbers in your birth date. First, begin by reducing the month, day, and year numbers of your birth date down to three single-digit numbers unless they total 11 or 22. If you have an 11 or 22 month, day, or year—that is, if you were born in November (11); on the 11th, 22nd, or 29th of your birth month; or in a year that totals 11 or 22, such as 1975 (1 + 9 + 7 + 5 = 22)—it doesn't reduce down to 2 or 4 but rather remains 11 or 22.

> **Please Note:** *At this stage of the equation some numerologists will reduce 11 and 22 down to 2 and 4, so you'll have to go with your gut on this one and do whatever feels right for you. In the example below I am leaving the 11 as it is.*

Let's use the birth date December 11, 1969 (12-11-1969), as an example once again, and the three single-digits 3, 11, and 7 to calculate the four Pinnacle Numbers:

12 / 11 / 1969
1+2 11 1+9+6+9 = 25
  3 11   2+5
               7

First Pinnacle Number

Month of birth + day of birth

3+11 = 14
1+4 = **5 Pinnacle**

The first Pinnacle focuses on self-discovery and self-realization.

Second Pinnacle Number

Day of birth + year of birth

11+7 = 18
1+8 = **9 Pinnacle**

The second Pinnacle focuses on responsibility and relationships with others.

Third Pinnacle Number

First Pinnacle Number + Second Pinnacle Number

5 Pinnacle + 9 Pinnacle = 14
1+4 = **5 Pinnacle**

The third Pinnacle focuses on maturity and preparation for the fourth and final Pinnacle.

Fourth Pinnacle Number

Month of birth + year of birth

3+7 = 10
1+0 = 1 **Pinnacle**

The fourth Pinnacle focuses on reflection, wisdom, and self-mastery.

Please note: *If you end up with a Pinnacle Number 11, 22, or 33, it becomes an 11/2, 22/4, or 33/6 Pinnacle Number and does not get reduced down, although some numerologists reduce the 33/6 down to a 6 Pinnacle Number.*

How to Calculate Your Pinnacle Periods

First Pinnacle Period

Subtract your Life Path Number from 36.
The First Pinnacle Period is from birth (age 0) until the age of your Life Path Number subtracted from 36.
For example, the First Pinnacle Period for a 3 Life Path would be 0 to 33 years because 3 subtracted from 36 is 33.

Please note: *When it comes to Life Path Number 11/2, some numerologists subtract 11 from 36, making the First Pinnacle Period age 0 to 25 years; and some subtract 2, making it 0 to 34 years. The same applies for Life Path 10/1. Some numerologists subtract 10 from 36, making the First Pinnacle Period age 0 to 26 years; and some subtract 1, making it 0 to 35 years. Once again, it's a matter of personal preference. In the case of Life Path 22/4, all numerologists subtract 4, making the First Pinnacle Period age 0 to 32 years. For Life Path 33/6, all numerologists subtract 6, making the First Pinnacle Period 0 to 30 years.*

Why 36? By subtracting every Life Path Number from 36, it ensures that each Pinnacle period finishes on a 9 Personal Year (described in the next section), a year of endings and completion, in preparation for new beginnings (1 Personal Year).

Second Pinnacle Period

The Second Pinnacle Period is nine years in duration and commences when the previous period ends.

For example, the Second Pinnacle Period for a 3 Life Path begins at age 34 and continues for 9 years until the 43rd birthday.

Third Pinnacle Period

The Third Pinnacle Period is nine years in duration also and commences when the previous period ends.

For example, the Third Pinnacle Period for a 3 Life Path begins at age 43 and continues for 9 years until the 52nd birthday.

Fourth Pinnacle Period

The Fourth Pinnacle Period starts where the third period ends and continues until the end of your life.

For example, the Fourth Pinnacle Period for a 3 Life Path begins at age 52 and continues until the time of passing.

✵

Now let's take a look at the Pinnacle Number meanings.

Pinnacle Number Meanings

1 Pinnacle Number

Independence, Courage, Individuality, Leadership

This Pinnacle provides the opportunity to become self-sufficient, independent, and confident. During this cycle, you'll learn to make your own decisions, be assertive, and stand on your own two feet. In most cases, you're being groomed for a leadership role; however, you can only be an effective leader of others when you've fully mastered yourself. To make the most of this Pinnacle, you must embrace your individuality and overcome your fear of others' opinions. This Pinnacle will motivate you to achieve your goals.

2 Pinnacle Number

Sensitivity, Intuition, Cooperation, Balance

This Pinnacle provides the opportunity to harmonize more effectively with others through cooperation and compromise. During this cycle, you'll learn to embrace your sensitivity and balance your emotions. You will also learn to balance giving with receiving, intuition with logic, and your personal life with your career. You have the desire and ability to influence others energetically and verbally during this time, and you may feel drawn to healing, creative, or musical pursuits. To make the most of this Pinnacle, you must focus on your strengths rather than your shortcomings and believe that you're worthy of greatness. This Pinnacle will enable you to form meaningful relationships with others due to a deeper understanding and awareness.

3 Pinnacle Number

Creativity, Self-Expression, Social Activity, Joy

This Pinnacle provides the opportunity to express yourself verbally and creatively. You may even pursue a communication-based career while under this vibration. There is much potential for artistic achievement during this time, so put your creative talents to good use. During this cycle, you'll learn to communicate more effectively with others by learning to identify your feelings so you can put those feelings into words. This enables you to have your say and speak your truth. To make the most of this Pinnacle, you must use your creative gifts to inspire others and yourself. This is a fun and favorable cycle where you'll form many friendships and lead an active social life.

4 Pinnacle Number

Building, Planning, Effort, Discipline, Focus

This Pinnacle provides the opportunity to build a solid foundation for your future. During this cycle, you'll learn to organize yourself and others and persist through adversity to achieve your goals. You'll discover the importance of planning, responsibility, and self-discipline so you can build something of lasting value. To make the most of this Pinnacle, try to be optimistic and see the light at the end of the tunnel. No matter how hard things may seem, you must never, ever give up. This Pinnacle will enable you to set yourself up for life through dedication and hard work.

5 Pinnacle Number

Exploration, Experience, Freedom, Communication

This Pinnacle provides the opportunity to explore the world around you and experiment with life. You'll experience an increase in personal freedom during this time, and many interesting people and opportunities will continue to cross your path. You'll discover the importance of moderation, self-discipline, and focus in order to achieve your goals, but to make the most of this Pinnacle, you must take a calculated risk and think outside the box. This Pinnacle will enable you to promote yourself and your message and communicate more effectively with others. There will be many changes and unexpected events during this time, so prepare for plenty of action.

6 Pinnacle Number

Love, Family, Domestic Responsibility, Creativity

This Pinnacle provides the opportunity to love and be loved while defining your personal boundaries. During this cycle, you'll learn about love in its many forms—from romantic love to love of family and friends—and all the relationship highs and lows that go hand in hand. Even though you'll feel a strong sense of responsibility toward others, you must learn to balance others' needs with your own. To make the most of this Pinnacle, you must be available to those in need and make time for yourself as well. This Pinnacle will help you be of service to others without becoming a doormat or martyr.

7 Pinnacle Number

Introspection, Specialization, Spirituality, Personal Growth

This Pinnacle provides the opportunity to work on your personal development and gain a deeper understanding of life. During this cycle, you'll want to spend quiet time alone in contemplation to find your spiritual truth, as doing so will improve your circumstances in the outer world. To make the most of this Pinnacle, you must trust your intuition and enhance your connection to the Divine with regular prayer and meditation, yoga, conscious breathing, and/or qigong. Spending time in nature (especially around water) will help raise your vibration and improve your connection to Source (that is, the Universe, God, the Divine, or whatever you choose to call this force). This is the perfect time to study and become a specialist in your craft.

8 Pinnacle Number

Personal Power, Manifestation, Finances, Career

This Pinnacle provides the opportunity to reclaim your personal power and confront whatever causes you to feel *dis*empowered. During this cycle, you'll learn about business and financial affairs and may even start your own business. Provided that you put in the effort, adopt an attitude of abundance, and live with honesty and integrity at all times, there is much potential for recognition and success. To make the most of this Pinnacle, you must be positive and have a healthy relationship with money. When you recognize that success, money, image, and power don't define you, you will actualize your dreams.

9 Pinnacle Number

Compassion, Humanitarianism, Service, Creativity

This Pinnacle provides the opportunity to develop broadmindedness and compassion toward others. Although it may be challenging at times, you'll come out the other end with greater tolerance, wisdom, and an appreciation of life. To make the most of this Pinnacle, you must forgive yourself and others, and let go of anything in your life that no longer serves you. When you release the need to control your environment and surrender to the universal flow of life, your success is guaranteed. This Pinnacle will increase your humanitarian desires and enhance your creative abilities so you can flourish in the arts.

11/2 Pinnacle Number

Inspiration, Illumination, Transformation, Spiritual Awakening

Also read the description for 2 Pinnacle Number.

This Pinnacle provides the opportunity to master your sensitivity and intuition. With effort and determination, you'll learn to remain centered and grounded at all times and balance your emotions, which is a requirement to harness the intense vibration of the 11/2. An 11/2 Pinnacle focuses on building enough self-confidence, wisdom, and compassion to handle its demands. To make the most of this Pinnacle, you must work on improving yourself and living by your higher ideals. Despite the many tests, trials, and tribulations, there is much potential for success. This Pinnacle will enable you to reach a higher level of consciousness, understand universal laws, and inspire others with ease.

22/4 Pinnacle Number

Commitment, Achievement, Establishment, Spiritual Awakening

Also read the description for 4 Pinnacle Number.

This Pinnacle provides the opportunity to implement, manage, or support a large-scale endeavor that serves the community or humanity as a whole. During this cycle, you have the ability to manifest ideas into physical form through practical action, discipline, and a higher awareness. To make the most of this Pinnacle, you must learn to soothe your nerves, balance your emotions, and stay grounded at all times while you dedicate yourself entirely to your goals. This is a time to dream big, but you must have the faith, courage, and stamina to follow through. This Pinnacle will enable you to build, create, or promote something that has a lasting impact on the world.

33/6 Pinnacle Number

Love, Healing, Selfless Service, Spiritual Awakening

Also read the description for 6 Pinnacle Number.

This Pinnacle provides the opportunity to utilize your powerful healing energy through unconditional love. During this cycle, you'll learn not to personalize the pain you see in the world while you seek to serve the greater good. This is a challenging cycle that entails great sacrifice and responsibility; however, there is much potential to make a difference in the world. To make the most of this Pinnacle, you must utilize your creative abilities and ensure that you remain balanced, grounded, and semi-detached at all times. This Pinnacle will enable you to heal with love and elevate the consciousness of humanity through selfless service.

CHALLENGES

Where the Pinnacles indicate four potential areas of achievement, the Challenges identify four specific obstacles that must be overcome in order to reach your full potential. As you journey toward self-mastery, your Challenge Numbers represent the lessons you must learn in order to expand your awareness and improve your quality of life.

Since the Pinnacle periods and Challenge periods are the same, each Challenge Number runs in conjunction with a Pinnacle Number. When you choose to rise to the occasion and face the Challenge head-on, you reap the full benefit of its accompanying Pinnacle. In other words, you'll experience a more successful Pinnacle period when you overcome the Challenge that accompanies it. You can think of your Pinnacles and Challenges as your strengths and weaknesses during a specific period of time.

When you understand the nature of your Challenge Number and do your best to overcome it (rather than ignore or avoid it), you're living in harmony with your numbers and the universal flow of life. This, in turn, attracts a more harmonious life experience. You have free will at all times to avoid the Challenges that are presented to you; however, what you resist, persists, so your Challenges will continue to seek you out. There's no escaping these Challenges, for they will continually present themselves to you throughout your life until you face them once and for all. So it's best to just bite the bullet and get on with it.

If you want to improve your quality of life and enhance your ability to manifest your dreams, you must face your Challenges with courage and determination. However hard it seems, always remember that no souls are given more than they can handle. Even when you're in the depths of despair, you must know and believe in your heart that you were born with the strength and ability to make it through every one of your Challenges.

How to Calculate Your Challenge Numbers

The four Challenge Numbers are calculated from the month, day, and year of your birth date.

The only difference between calculating the Pinnacle and Challenge Numbers is that we use *addition* for the Pinnacles and *subtraction* for the Challenges. Because we're subtracting numbers, it's perfectly normal to end up with a 0 or negative (–) Challenge Number.

First, we begin by reducing the month, day, and year numbers of your birth date down to three single-digit numbers.

Please note: *When calculating Challenge Numbers, the majority of numerologists reduce 11 and 22 down to single-digit numbers 2 and 4, while some choose to keep them as 11 and 22.*

For example, if you were born in November or on the 11th day of the month, both the month and day numbers would reduce down to 2.

Let's use December 11, 1969 (12-11-1969), as an example once again:

147

12 / 11 / 1969
1+2 1+1 1+9+6+9 = 25
  3   2   2+5
                   7

Therefore, the three single digits for birth date 12-11-1969 are 3, 2, and 7.

Follow the formulas below to calculate your four Challenge Numbers.

First Challenge Number

Month of birth – (minus) day of birth (or find the difference by subtracting the smaller number from the larger).

For example:

3–2 = 1 Challenge Number

This Challenge Number will influence you during the first Challenge Number period and focuses on the early part of your life.

Second Challenge Number

Day of birth – (minus) year of birth (or find the difference by subtracting the smaller number from the larger).

For example:

2–7 = 5 Challenge Number

Rather than have a –5 answer, we would find the difference between 2 and 7 by subtracting the smaller number from the larger number, giving us a 5 Challenge Number.

This Challenge Number will influence you during the second Challenge Number period and focuses on the middle part of your life.

Third Challenge Number

Find the difference between the First and Second Challenge Numbers.

For example:

1–5 = 4 Challenge Number

Rather than have a –4 answer, we would find the difference between 1 and 5 by subtracting the smaller number from the larger number, giving us a 4 Challenge Number.

This Challenge Number is considered your main Challenge and will not only influence you during your third Challenge Number period; it will influence you throughout the entire course of your life. This will be your most demanding Challenge of all.

Fourth Challenge Number

Month of birth – year of birth (or find the difference by subtracting the smaller number from the larger).

For example:

3–7 = 4 Challenge Number

Rather than have a −4 answer, we would find the difference between 3 and 7 by subtracting the smaller number from the larger number, giving us a 4 Challenge Number.

This Challenge Number will influence you during the fourth Challenge Number period and focuses on your middle-to-late years until the end of your life.

Please note: *Some numerologists disregard the Fourth Challenge Number altogether and focus only upon the first three.*

It is not uncommon for a Challenge Number to repeat itself in a chart.

How to Calculate Your Challenge Periods

Your Challenge Number periods are the same as your Pinnacle Number periods.

❋

Now let's take a look at the Challenge Number meanings.

Challenge Number Meanings

0 Challenge Number

The 0 Challenge Number is a challenge of *choice,* where it's your decision to choose whether to live to your highest potential or to simply cruise along. Because of the free-will aspect, a 0 Challenge can be extremely challenging or not very challenging at all—it all depends on which path you choose. One thing is for certain: a 0 Challenge doesn't indicate a challenge-free life, as there are challenges to be faced through the other numbers in your chart. It does, however, indicate an opportunity to attain a higher level of awareness and understanding through many profound life experiences. During this cycle, you'll be challenged to devote yourself to a greater cause and express unconditional love to all. This is where you're in the driver's seat of life and will be challenged to make decisions that serve others as well as yourself.

1 Challenge Number

During this cycle, you'll be challenged to embrace your independence and stand on your own two feet. This is vital to your success if you want to make your way in the world. There will be times when you'll feel like a square peg in a round hole and will need to embrace your individuality in order to experience a sense of belonging. Should you ever feel disempowered, this cycle will encourage you to stand up for yourself and your beliefs. It will also encourage you to become more self-aware so you can build your confidence and trust your intuition and judgment. This Challenge is designed to help you strengthen your willpower and utilize your creative mind. This is where you learn to become a leader rather than follow the crowd.

2 Challenge Number

This cycle will challenge you to cooperate with others and resolve conflict peacefully. Since 2 represents the emotions, you may feel hypersensitive and self-conscious during this cycle, so you'll need to stabilize yourself from within by working on your self-confidence and balancing your emotions. *Balance* is the main focus of this Challenge; you'll be encouraged to balance giving with receiving, intuition with logic, and your personal life with your career. You'll also be challenged to define your personal limits and boundaries so you can learn to say no. Your heightened sensitivity enables you to care deeply for others; however, it can also create an exaggerated fear of criticism. During this cycle, you'll be challenged to have confidence in yourself and express your emotions in a healthy way.

3 Challenge Number

During this cycle, you'll be challenged to identify your feelings and put them into words that enable you to speak your truth. This Challenge focuses on communication and self-expression, where you'll learn that your words are affirmations that must be chosen carefully. During this cycle, you'll be challenged to express your words positively to uplift and inspire others, rather than negatively to exaggerate, gossip, or complain. Number 3 is a scattered energy, so you'll be encouraged to focus and prioritize. You'll learn that having your finger in too many pies achieves minimal results. Regular creative self-expression will make this Challenge easier. This cycle will inspire you to lighten up and experience more joy.

4 Challenge Number

This cycle will challenge you to live with restrictions and limitations, yet still achieve your goals. Extra mental, emotional, and physical effort will be required; however, your mind-set is the key to accomplishing the outcome you desire. During this cycle, you'll learn to be patient, organized, and responsible. You'll discover that your recipe for success is using a step-by-step process to gradually attain what you desire. Your major lesson during this Challenge is to be positive and to see the light at the end of the tunnel despite the obstacles and delays that prevent you from moving forward. Perseverance, discipline, and focus will help you overcome this Challenge, and your attitude determines your success.

5 Challenge Number

This cycle will challenge you to balance your quest for personal freedom with your need to fulfill your obligations. Despite your desire to throw caution to the wind, you'll learn to be accountable for your actions and take your responsibilities seriously. This cycle will also challenge you to rise above your inclination to overindulge your senses. If you're addicted to alcohol, food, sex, gambling, or spending—or prone to obsessive behavior—this Challenge will encourage you to exercise temperance and moderation. It will also teach you to step outside your comfort zone to experience new things; however, you must learn to channel your energy in one direction. Movement and change are associated with the number 5, and this cycle will teach you how to be flexible and adaptable and go with the flow.

6 Challenge Number

This cycle will challenge you to accept the imperfection in others, yourself, and the world. During this Challenge, you'll learn to accept things as they are, because it's impossible for anyone or anything to live up to your idealistic standards. This cycle will also challenge you to define your personal limits and boundaries and balance others' needs with your own. Despite only wanting the best for people, you will have to avoid the temptation to interfere unnecessarily in their lives. One of your greatest lessons during this time is to learn to say no, because the failure to do so can result in martyrdom and frustration. Because 6 represents family, you'll be challenged to take your familial responsibilities seriously and to make yourself available to those in need. During this cycle, extra effort may be required to build harmonious relationships; however, the key to success is knowing that the "perfect" person, marriage, and family doesn't exist.

7 Challenge Number

This cycle will challenge you to *trust*—in yourself, others, the process of life, a higher power, and the unknown. This Challenge is much easier when you adopt a spiritual faith. Without a sense of connection to the whole, there are times when you may feel isolated and alone; therefore, this Challenge will encourage you to discover your spiritual truth. During this cycle, you'll also be encouraged to open up to others and to reach out to them for assistance. Despite how frightening it can be, you must learn to trust and take a leap of faith. Rather than hide behind logic, superficiality, and bravado, you will be encouraged to express your thoughts and emotions. When you focus on your personal development and the higher meaning of life, you'll rise above this Challenge and improve your quality of life. This cycle will also challenge you to hone your craft.

8 Challenge Number

This cycle will challenge you to adopt an attitude of abundance and to balance the material and spiritual worlds. During this cycle, you'll learn to develop a healthy relationship with money while knowing that your finances, power, image, and status do not define you. To rise above this Challenge, you'll need to believe that the Universe is abundant, yet overcome your obsession with money and the accumulation of material goods. If you struggle to make ends meet, this Challenge will teach you that your mind-set is the key to financial stability and job satisfaction. Because 8 is governed by the Law of Cause and Effect, honesty, integrity, and a good work ethic are the keys to your success. This Challenge will also encourage you to reclaim your personal power over anything or anyone that takes your power away.

Please take note of your Challenges, but don't dwell on them. Despite how challenging your life may be, try to remember that your soul has chosen these Challenges in advance because you have the inner strength and ability to make it through. Never underestimate the power and wisdom of your soul—and call upon your higher self anytime you need a helping hand. Also, remember to call on God, your spirit guides, angels, and loved ones in spirit for extra assistance when needed.

PERSONAL YEAR NUMBER

Falling directly under the Pinnacles and Challenges is the Personal Year Cycle, one of the most significant life cycles in your chart. Your Personal Year Cycle commences at birth and progresses through nine-year intervals throughout your life. For the duration of one year, you have a *Personal Year Number* between 1 and 9 (or Master Number 11/2 or 22/4), which contains the lessons, opportunities, and experiences you'll encounter during the course of that year.

Most numerologists believe that the Personal Year Number runs from January 1 to December 31 because it coincides with the calendar-year cycle, while others believe it runs from birthday to birthday. As with all conflicting theories in numerology, neither is right or wrong—they're just different and come down to personal preference. I suggest you calculate your Personal Month Numbers (which we'll cover in the following segment) for the past 12 months using both systems to determine which is more accurate for you.

With all numerology cycles, the influence of a new cycle number can begin prior to the official changeover date. Depending on your month of birth, the new Personal Year Number energy can be felt up to several months prior to January 1. For those with birthdays toward the end of the year, the new Personal Year Number may not be felt until several months after January 1.

The Personal Year Cycle is a nine-year cycle of personal growth where each Personal Year Number has a unique theme with respect to the types of lessons and experiences you'll encounter for that year. Because *a number has the same meaning wherever it appears,* you'll find that the Personal Year Number meanings are similar to other cycle number meanings such as the Major Life Cycle, Pinnacle, Personal Month, and Essence Numbers (which I'll address a little further on); however, the Personal Year Number has the strongest influence of all for the year.

When you know your Personal Year Number, you can prepare for the potential challenges and opportunities coming your way. Your Personal Year Number is also a great indicator of the ideal time to take certain actions, such as focusing on your career; moving, traveling, or taking an adventure; repairing, ending, or beginning a relationship; studying; getting married; working on your personal development; or starting a family.

When you know the Personal Year Number of those around you, you'll have a better understanding of what's going on in their lives, too, which in turn improves your relationships immensely. Even though you may not be in the same Personal Year Number and may experience different lessons, viewpoints, and opportunities during the year, when you know which direction your loved one is heading, you can be ready for what's ahead. For example, if you know that your partner is in an 8 Personal Year, you know that he or she is going to be focusing on financial and career objectives. Knowing this in advance means you can be supportive of his or her quest to save and make money or to gain recognition on the job. Or, if you know that your partner is in a 7 Personal Year, you know that he or she is going to want to spend more quiet time alone. You can then give him or her the necessary time and space and not take it as a personal rejection of your company.

Your Personal Year Number is greatly influenced by your Essence, Personal Month, Major Life Cycle, Pinnacle, and Challenge Numbers. In fact, the key to an accurate forecast lies in blending all of these numbers (energies/influences) together and adding the Universal Year Number to the mix.

The Universal Year Number (also known as the World Year Number) is the total of the current calendar year. For example: 2014 (2 + 0 + 1 + 4) = 7 Universal Year Number. You can think of the Universal Year Number as the Personal Year Number for the world, which influences humanity as a whole regardless of each individual's Personal Year Number.

Because *a number has the same meaning wherever it appears,* the Universal Year Numbers have the same meanings as the Personal Year Numbers, except they apply to the world rather than an individual. When you take the Universal Year Number into consideration alongside the other cycle numbers in your chart, you cover all your bases and form a deeper understanding of what is going on around you.

Here is a brief outline of the Universal Year Number meanings:

- **1 Universal Year Number**—New Beginnings and Action

- **2 Universal Year Number**—Cooperation and Balance

- **3 Universal Year Number**—Communication and Expression

- **4 Universal Year Number**—Building and Planning

- **5 Universal Year Number**—Movement and Change

- **6 Universal Year Number**—Responsibility and Universal Love

- **7 Universal Year Number**—Introspection and Personal Growth

- **8 Universal Year Number**—Karmic Justice and Power

- **9 Universal Year Number**—Endings and Completions

- **11/2 Universal Year Number**—Illumination and Higher Learning

- **22/4 Universal Year Number**—Accomplishment and Transformation

How to Calculate Your Personal Year Number

The Personal Year Number is calculated by adding the month and day of your birth date to the Universal Year Number.

Adding-Across Method

Step 1: To find your Personal Year Number for any given year, add the month and day of your birth date to the Universal Year Number of inquiry.

Step 2: Add any double-digit numbers together to get a single-digit Personal Year Number unless they total 11 or 22, which becomes an 11/2 or 22/4 Personal Year Number. Remember to write the complete year number—that is, 2014 rather than just 14.

To find the 2014 Personal Year Number for Mary Ann Smith, born December 11, 1969, the calculation would be:

1+2+1+1+2+0+1+4 = 12
1+2 = **3 Personal Year Number**

To find out what Mary Ann Smith's Personal Year Number was back in 2008, the calculation would be:

1+2+1+1+2+0+0+8 = 15
1+5 = **6 Personal Year Number in 2008**

Sometimes you may end up with an 11/2 or 22/4 Personal Year Number, as in the below example for birth date March 1, 1960:

3+1+2+0+1+4 = **11/2 Personal Year Number**

Please Note: *Some numerologists acknowledge Personal Year Numbers 11/2 and 22/4, and some don't. I believe Personal Year Numbers 11/2 and 22/4 are higher-octave vibrations of*

Personal Years 2 and 4 that provide additional opportunities for spiritual awakening and personal transformation; however, we have free will as to whether we'll choose to take the opportunity or not.

Reducing-Down Method

Some numerologists prefer the reducing-down method for calculating the Personal Year Number.

Step 1: Reduce the month, day, and Universal Year Number down to three single-digit numbers, as shown below:

> **Please Note:** *At this point of the calculation, some numerologists will reduce an 11 or 22 birth month, day, or year down to a 2 or 4, and others don't. It's up to you which method you prefer to use. I'll leave the 11 as it is in this example.*
>
> 1+2 / 11 / 2+0+1+4
> 3   11   7

Step 2: Add the single totals (and 11 and 22 where applicable) together and continue to reduce down until you get a single-digit Personal Year Number, unless they total 11 or 22, which becomes an 11/2 or 22/4 Personal Year Number.

> 3+11+7 = 21
> 2+1 = **3 Personal Year Number**

✻

Now let's take a look at the Personal Year Number meanings.

Personal Year Number Meanings

1 Personal Year Number

New Beginnings, Action, Opportunity

Where last year was about completion and letting go, this is a year of new beginnings and opportunities to create a fresh start. This is an action-packed year where you must find the courage to make the necessary changes that will improve your quality of life. Whether it involves embarking upon a new relationship, begin-ning a new career, or moving into a new home, this is a time to go for it and take the bull by the horns. Don't let your fears and insecurities hold you back. Feel the fear and do it anyway, and take a leap of faith.

This is also a year to embrace your individuality and indepen-dence—to stand on your own two feet and march to the beat of your own drum. By doing things *your* way rather than following the crowd, you'll improve your chance for success. You'll have in-creased faith in your judgment and intuition this year, so be pro-active and follow through with any life-changing decisions you make. Number 1 is about being unique and one of a kind, so be proud of who you are and be sure to follow your dreams even if they seem out of reach or go against others' desires for you. This is the year to make yourself #1 and do what's right for *you*.

This is the perfect year to create a new you by having a make-over, working on your personal development, taking up a new hobby, beginning a healthy new lifestyle, or simply adopting a positive mind-set. As 1 is a powerful manifestation number, the seeds you plant this year will set the tone for the next nine years. So be optimistic about yourself and your future, focus only on your strengths, and set out to achieve your goals.

2 Personal Year Number

Relationships, Balance, Emotions

Self-love and your relationship with yourself is your first priority this year as you work on building your confidence and healing whatever needs to be healed. This is a year to achieve mental and emotional balance by addressing any unresolved emotions or limiting beliefs that are preventing you from living a happy, harmonious life. This is also a year to create harmony in your life by balancing your intuition with logic, your home life with your career, giving with receiving, and others' needs with your own.

This is also a year where relationship issues that have been brewing with work colleagues, family, friends, or partners will come to the surface in order to be resolved. Therefore, it pays to be cooperative, tolerant, understanding, and diplomatic at all times. Because 2 represents partnership and meaningful connections with others, this is a wonderful year to solidify the relationships in your life. It's also a very favorable year for singles to find love—bearing in mind that healthy relationships with others can only stem from a healthy relationship with oneself.

This year can bring about exaggerated emotions and extrasensory experiences, so you may feel hypersensitive to criticism and overreact at times. Your intuition is heightened, so follow your inner guidance and you'll automatically be led where you need to be. This is a time to create a harmonious environment, take up meditation, create or listen to beautiful music, enhance your psychic abilities, spend time in nature, and eat healthy food. This is a slow and steady year of adaptability that requires patience. When you let go and go with the flow, it can be a very rewarding time. Number 2 is governed by the moon, so work closely with the lunar cycles throughout the year to assist in manifesting your dreams. (See "Moon Cyles" in the "Manifestation with Numbers" section in Part III.)

161

3 Personal Year Number

Self-Expression, Communication, Creativity

This year focuses on self-expression, whether it's of an artistic nature or communication of the spoken or written word. Either way, this is a favorable time to speak your truth and express your feelings through honest conversation, art, creative writing, or journaling (if you prefer to keep things to yourself). In order to make the most of this year, you need to let your feelings out.

Number 3 intensifies emotions, so if you're dwelling on the negative or focusing on unnecessary drama, things can become a lot worse than they are and spiral out of control. Therefore, it pays to lighten up and have fun in a 3 year, and try to see the glass half-full. This is the perfect time to take a vacation, socialize with old friends, make *new* friends, and partake in joyful activities. Any form of creative expression is favored this year—whether it's painting, dancing, gardening, writing, photography, jewelry making, sewing, cooking, decorating, or designing. As long as it feels good, you're on the right path.

As 3 is a scattered energy, you may be easily bored and distracted this year, so try not to take on too many things at once. Keep things simple; prioritize your goals; and stay organized, disciplined, and focused to make the most of this year. Be responsible, plan your finances carefully, and try to finish any existing projects before starting anything new.

4 Personal Year Number

Effort, Building, Planning

This year is all about building a solid foundation for your future by putting systems in place that will help you improve your quality of life. For example, if you're thinking of selling your home, this is the year to make property improvements and repairs in preparation for the sale. Or, if you'd like to start a business, this is a year to search for a location, build your client base, and develop your website. Think of this year as laying the groundwork to set yourself up for life.

This can be a year of hard work, as 4 indicates that extra physical, mental, and emotional effort is required to obtain your desired results. So prioritize your time and face your challenges head-on. Now, it may take longer than usual for things to come to fruition and to reap the rewards of your efforts; however, the lesson of the 4 is to be patient and persevere through obstacles and delays. No matter hard it gets, never, ever give up! Think of this year as a test of your dedication and commitment to yourself, where your attitude is the key to your success.

Physical, mental, emotional, and financial stability are essential this year, so focus on your health, be optimistic, deal with issues from the past, avoid unnecessary drama and confrontation with others, and plan your finances carefully. With dedication, determination, and discipline, you'll be rewarded for your efforts.

5 Personal Year Number

Progress, Movement, Change

This is a dynamic and action-packed year, full of expected and unexpected change. Anything can happen, and it usually does with number 5, so use this to your advantage by being adventurous, taking calculated risks, and experiencing new things. This is a year of progress and freedom compared to the constraints of last year; however, whether it's an exciting or chaotic year depends upon your attitude. Extra effort is required to eliminate unnecessary drama from your life. Your key to success in a 5 year is to be adaptable and flexible and to go with the flow. Expect the unexpected, and don't make plans set in stone.

This is a year to get out and about, travel, visit new places, and make new friends. You'll have the gift of gab, so it's the ideal time to promote yourself and make your message known. Given that 5 is a scattered energy, extra effort is required to remain focused, grounded, and stable. Try not to take on too many things at once or you'll accomplish very little and things can spiral out of control. You'll learn the importance of freedom, coupled with moderation, throughout the course of this year.

Temperance and discipline are essential this year, so be mindful not to overindulge your senses by overeating, drinking too much, or partaking in other excessive behaviors. Try not to get caught up in life's dramas, and focus on making positive changes that will improve your quality of life. Whether it's a lifestyle or relationship change—or change of residence, attitude, or career—this is a year of movement and progress toward bigger and better things.

6 Personal Year Number

Love, Family, Domestic Responsibility

This year is all about responsibility and sacrifice. Your relationships with friends, family, and loved ones will require your attention. During the course of this year, you'll need to balance your career with your domestic responsibilities and find the middle ground between giving to others and honoring your own needs. You will also need to take responsibility for your actions.

This is a very favorable time for singles to find romance, as 6 is the love number. If you're already in a relationship or married, issues that have been brewing will rise to the surface to be resolved. Typically, this is a year where couples either make up or break up. Therefore, this is the perfect opportunity to take your relationship to a deeper level of commitment and understanding or else to go your separate ways. Regardless, this is the year to make every relationship in your life the best it can be.

This is an opportune time for those working in the healing arts or in a service-based career, because when you focus on being of service, you'll be given plenty of opportunities to serve. In addition, 6 represents the home, so this is a good time to buy, sell, move, renovate, or decorate your living space. This is also a year to focus on your health, make a commitment, get married, or start a family. By honoring your responsibilities and being there for those in need, you could turn this into a very fruitful year.

7 Personal Year Number

Introspection, Personal and Spiritual Growth

This is a year to slow down and take a step back to focus on your inner development. You may not feel as motivated and social as you usually are and may prefer to spend quiet time alone to contemplate the meaning of life. This is the year where you'll ask the big questions: *Who am I? Where is my life going?* and *What is my life purpose?* As you ponder these questions, the answers that arise will change the course of your life. This is a year where the more *inner* work you do, the greater your success in the *outer* world.

Your capacity for research and understanding is at its peak throughout the year; therefore, it's a favorable time to study— especially anything that relates to metaphysics, analytics, philosophy, science, computers and technology, psychology, or conventional or alternative health. This is also a year to discover the secrets and mysteries of the Universe and investigate anything that falls under the umbrella of "mind-body-spirit." Regular meditation, prayer, and spending quality time in nature and the outdoors will also be of great benefit this year.

During the course of the year, you'll find yourself being led to the perfect book, therapy approach, or workshop that will catapult you toward your next level of development. You may start practicing a faith, take up yoga or qigong, learn EFT (tapping), detox, start juicing, get an energy healing, or have a spiritual reading, since this is the year to enhance your connection to Source (God, Universe, Divine) and discover your spiritual truth. This is also a year to build a strong inner foundation in preparation for the years to come. In fact, your future success depends upon the improvements you make today.

8 Personal Year Number

Personal Power, Finances, Career

This year focuses on business, career, property, finances, and legal matters. For some there will be opportunities for recognition, expansion, and financial gain, while others may experience a reversal of fortune or financial loss. As 8 is the number of karmic balance, the outcome of this year is often in proportion to your life lessons, along with your efforts, attitude, and intentions over the past seven years. You'll reap what you've sown in an 8 year, and if you've been honest, hardworking, and considerate, you'll be rewarded in some way.

This is also a year to reclaim your personal power by asserting yourself when dealing with authority and confronting anything or anyone that has disempowered you in some way. Whether it's an overpowering person, addiction, fear, or belief, this is the year to confront it once and for all and take ownership of your power.

Money and manifestation are part of the energy of number 8, so get your finances in order and be mindful not to overspend. In order to attract abundance and opportunity, you'll need to balance the material and spiritual worlds and learn that money, image, appearance, status, and power don't define you.

This is a powerful cycle of manifestation where you can attract what you focus on the most, so focus on the positives and minimize your fears. This is a very karmic year where major lessons will be learned, and important connections will be made. Significant people will cross your path who can enhance your career or your overall quality of life. Since 8 governs the Law of Cause and Effect, it's essential that you live with honesty and integrity at all times.

9 Personal Year Number

Transformation, Completion, Endings

As this is the final year in a nine-year cycle, it focuses on completion and transformation in preparation for new beginnings. A major part of this transformation involves letting go of the things in your life that no longer serve you—whether it's a job, friendship, relationship, residence, mind-set, or behavior you may have outgrown. Either way, this is a time to spring-clean your life so you can move toward better things.

This can be an emotional year for those who fear the unknown or who find it difficult to adapt to change. So try to be courageous, optimistic, and strong, and know that all is well. To make the most of this year, trust in the Divine plan; surrender to change; forgive others and yourself; and accept, let go, and move on when things don't go your way. Despite it being a year of endings, it's also a year of rebirth and compensation, where everything you've been striving for can finally come to fruition.

Compassion and forgiveness play a major role this year, so be open-minded toward others and resolve outstanding conflicts and disputes. This is also a year to focus on being of service and following humanitarian pursuits by donating your time, money, attention, or unwanted items to a good cause. Perhaps you could do something to assist the environment or offer a helping hand to a charity, person, family, or animal in need.

11/2 Personal Year Number

Illumination, Inspiration, Personal Growth

As 11/2 is a higher octave of number 2, also read the 2 Personal Year Number description for additional insight.

The 11/2 Personal Year includes all the attributes of a 2 Personal Year, but offers further opportunities to reach a higher level of awareness. If you find yourself at a crossroads, now is the time to follow your passion and take a leap of faith toward the unknown rather than cling to the safe and familiar. This is a powerful year for personal transformation, in which opportunities for growth and enlightenment will result in many unique and inspired ideas.

You'll have the ability to illuminate and inspire others with ease—especially if you seek to serve the greater good. You may experience many intuitive insights and psychic encounters during this time, but the high intensity of the Master 11/2 vibration will force you to master your sensitivity and self-doubt. This is the year to trust your inner guidance and overcome your fears once and for all. To make the most of this year, you must work on your personal development and live with integrity at all times. There is much potential for success when you aspire to your higher ideals.

22/4 Personal Year Number

Accomplishment, Commitment, Personal Growth

As 22/4 is a higher octave of number 4, also read the 4 Personal Year Number description for additional insight.

The 22/4 Personal Year includes all the attributes of a 4 Personal Year, but offers additional opportunities to create, build, or promote something of importance that serves the greater good. This is a year to dream big, commit to your goals, and follow through with practical action. Due to the high intensity of the Master 22/4 vibration, you'll be more capable of converting your ideas into physical accomplishments than ever before. If you live by your higher ideals and dedicate yourself to your dreams, this could be a very fruitful year. Even though this year will enable you to implement, manage, or support a large-scale endeavor that serves the community or humanity as a whole, due to the double 2 energy, you must manage your nerves and balance your emotions to stay grounded at all times. This is a powerful cycle of achievement, provided that you have the necessary self-confidence, wisdom, and maturity to succeed.

❋

Now let's take a look at the Personal Month Number.

PERSONAL MONTH NUMBER

Falling directly under the Personal Year Cycle is the Personal Month Cycle. Where your Personal Year Number reveals the influence of the year, the Personal Month Number reveals the influence of the month. You can think of your Personal Year Number as the grand theme of the year, and your Personal Month Numbers as the 12 mini-themes within that year. However, the energy of the Personal Year Number is stronger than the Personal Month Number and has the greatest influence of all.

The key to gaining the most insight into a particular month is to blend your Personal Year Number and Personal Month Number energies together and use your common sense to evaluate what this combination could mean. For example, in a 9 Personal Year of transformation, completion, and endings, June is a 6 Personal Month that focuses on relationships, family, and domestic responsibilities. When you blend them together, this could indicate a time to end an unhealthy relationship; resolve and release any outstanding issues with your partner, family or friends; or move to another home.

How to Calculate Your Personal Month Number

The Personal Month Number is calculated by adding the Personal Year Number and Calendar Month Number together.

First, find the Calendar Month Number for the month of inquiry in the following list:

Calendar Month Numbers	
January—1	July—7
February—2	August—8
March—3	September—9
April—4	October—1
May—5	November—2
June—6	December—3

Please note: *Most numerologists reduce November down to a 2 Calendar Month Number; however, some keep it as 11. It's up to you what you prefer to do.*

To find your Personal Month Number for any given month, add your Personal Year Number to the Calendar Month Number. Add any double-digit numbers together to get a single-digit Personal Month Number unless they total 11 or 22, which becomes an 11/2 or 22/4 Personal Month Number.

For example, if your Personal Year Number is 3, to find your Personal Month Number for June (which is a 6 Calendar Month Number), you would add 6 to 3. Therefore, June is a 9 Personal Month in a 3 Personal Year.

It also pays to take the Universal Year Number and Universal Month Number into consideration for added insight into what's going on around you. The Universal Month Number for any given month is found by adding the Universal Year Number to the Calendar Month Number of inquiry. For example, to find the Universal Month Number for September 2014, you would add 9 (September's Calendar Month Number) to 7 (the Universal Year Number for 2014):

$$\underline{9+7} = 16$$

You would then add any double-digit numbers together to get a single-digit Universal Month Number unless they total 11, which becomes an 11/2 Universal Month Number:

$$\underline{1+6} = 7 \text{ Universal Month Number}$$

Therefore, September 2014 is a 7 Universal Month in a 7 Universal Year.

Personal Month Number Meanings

Because *a number has the same meaning wherever it appears,* the Personal Month Numbers have the same meanings as the Personal Year Numbers, just with a milder intensity. The Universal Month Numbers have the same meanings, also, except they apply to the world rather than an individual. Refer to the Personal Year Number meanings for a reminder of what each Personal Month Number and Universal Month Number entails.

�֍

Now let's take a look at the Personal Day Number.

PERSONAL DAY NUMBER

Falling directly under the Personal Month Numbers are the Personal Day Numbers. That's right—every day of the month is a Personal Day Number. Even though the vibration of a Personal Day Number is extremely subtle and mild in comparison to the other cycle numbers in your chart, it pays to bear it in mind when making important decisions.

When evaluating your Personal Day Number, don't forget to take your Personal Year, Personal Month, and Essence Numbers (which I'll describe later), along with the Universal Year and Universal Month Numbers, into consideration. (*If* you can remember them all, that is!) By blending these numbers together, you can see the bigger picture of what's going on around you. When it comes to numerology forecasting, it's basically a matter of mix and match and blending everything together.

How to Calculate Your Personal Day Number

The Personal Day Number is calculated by adding the Personal Month Number and Calendar Day Number together.

To find your Personal Day Number for any given day, add your Personal Month Number to the Calendar Day Number of inquiry. Add any double-digit numbers together to get a single-digit Personal Day Number unless they total 11, which becomes an 11/2 Personal Day Number.

For example, if your Personal Month Number is 7, to find your Personal Day Number for the 2nd (which is a 2 Calendar Day Number), you would add 2 to 7. Therefore, the 2nd is 9 Personal Day in a 7 Personal Month.

Here's a list of the Calendar Day Numbers:

Calendar Day Numbers		
1st—1	11th—2	21st—3
2nd—2	12th—3	22nd—4
3rd—3	13th—4	23rd—5
4th—4	14th—5	24th—6
5th—5	15th—6	25th—7
6th—6	16th—7	26th—8
7th—7	17th—8	27th—9
8th—8	18th—9	28th—1
9th—9	19th—1	29th—2
10th—1	20th—2	30th—3
		31st—4

Please note: *Most numerologists reduce the 11th, 22nd, and 29th down to a 2 or 4 Calendar Day Number, whereas others don't reduce them beyond 11 and 22. It's up to you what you prefer to do.*

It also pays to take the Universal Day Number into consideration for added insight into what's going on around you.

To find the Universal Day Number, simply add the Universal Month Number to the Calendar Day Number of inquiry. Add any double-digit numbers together to get a single-digit Universal Day

Number unless they total 11, which becomes an 11/2 Universal Day Number.

For example, if the Universal Month Number is 3, to find the Universal Day Number for the 14th (which is a 5 Calendar Day Number), you would add 5 to 3. Therefore, the 14th is an 8 Universal Day in a 3 Universal Month.

The Universal Day Numbers have the same meanings as the Personal Day Numbers except they apply to the world rather than an individual.

Now let's take a look at the Personal Day Number meanings.

Personal Day Number Meanings

1 Personal Day Number

This is a day to begin something new, do something for yourself, be proactive, and take action.

2 Personal Day Number

This is a day to get in touch with your emotions, be cooperative and patient, and connect with others.

3 Personal Day Number

This is a day to have fun, catch up with friends, and express yourself verbally and creatively.

4 Personal Day Number

This is a day to work hard; do what needs to be done; and plan, focus, and get organized.

173

5 Personal Day Number

This is a day to make changes; communicate; teach and promote; and be social, adventurous, and free.

6 Personal Day Number

This is a day to focus on family, loved ones, and friends; be nurturing; and beautify yourself and your home.

7 Personal Day Number

This is a day to spend time alone, read, study, research, rest, meditate, pray, and connect with the Divine.

8 Personal Day Number

This is a day to focus on business, deal with legal matters, budget your finances, and be empowered.

9 Personal Day Number

This is a day to complete something, spring-clean, help others, make a donation, and be generous and compassionate.

11/2 Personal Day Number

Also read the description for 2 Personal Day Number.
This is a day to follow your intuition, heal or inspire someone (and/or yourself), and focus on your spiritual development.

It pays to be mindful when a Personal or Universal Year, Month, or Day Number is a Karmic Debt Number 13/4, 14/5, 16/7, or 19/1, as additional obstacles and challenges may present themselves. For a reminder of what those obstacles and challenges may be, reread the Karmic Debt Number descriptions in Part I.

✳

Now, let's move on to the Essence Number.

ESSENCE NUMBER

The Essence Number is a very important number that works in conjunction with the Personal Year Number and provides additional insight into what can be expected for the year. The Essence Number runs from birthday to birthday, and while you have a different Personal Year Number each year, there are occasions when you may have the same Essence Number for several years. On other occasions, you may have a different Essence Number altogether for several years in a row. It all depends on the letters in your original birth-certificate name.

Although your Personal Year Number reveals the *external* environment and influences outside of you, the Essence Number reveals your *internal* environment, such as your mind-set, needs, desires, and perspectives. Together, the Personal Year Number and Essence Number provide valuable information to help you understand your inner and outer environment at any given time. On the one hand, your Personal Year Number will reveal what's going on around you for the year, and on the other, your Essence Number will reveal your mind-set and perspective as the year unfolds.

When you add your Personal Month, Pinnacle, Challenge, and Major Life Cycle Numbers into the mix, you've got a handy guideline of the direction of your life and the energy that surrounds you. While the influence of all of these numbers can be felt, your Essence and Personal Year Numbers have the strongest influence.

You're guaranteed to feel the direct effects of your Essence Number and Personal Year Number over the course of the year, which is why it's important to understand what they are and what they represent. That way, you can make sense of your environment and have more control over your mind-set and behavior in order to achieve the best results.

To calculate your Essence Number, you must begin with an understanding of your Transits and the Table of Events, which I'll cover in the next two sections.

Transits

Whereas your Personal Year Number is calculated from your date of birth, the Essence Number is calculated from the letters in your original birth-certificate name. Each letter of your birth-certificate name has a specific duration and influence over your life, which is called a *Transit*. The duration of each Transit varies depending on the numerical value of the letter (see the Western letters-and-numbers chart in the "Table of Events" section to follow). For example, *D* is a 4 letter; therefore, the duration of a *D* transit is 4 years. There are three types of transits in a numerology chart: *physical, mental,* and *spiritual.*

Physical Transit

This Transit applies to the letters in your first name and influences the physical aspects of your life.

Mental Transit

This Transit applies to the letters in your middle name(s) and influences your mind-set and the mental aspects of your life. If you don't have a middle name, your Spiritual Transit Number also applies to your mind-set and the mental aspects of your life.

Spiritual Transit

This Transit applies to the letters in your last name and influences the spiritual aspects of your life.

✳

The Essence Number is the sum total of the Physical, Mental, and Spiritual Transits during any given year. Even though each Transit has an influence over your perspective and behavior, individually they're not as strong as the Essence Number total. With that being said, it still pays to take your individual Transit Numbers into consideration for greater understanding of your Essence Number forecast. The complete Transit and Essence Number chart of your life is called the *Table of Events.*

How to Assemble a Table of Events Chart

The Table of Events chart is calculated from your original birth-certificate name and the Western letters-and-numbers chart on the following page.

1	2	3	4	5	6	7	8	9
A	B	C	D	E	F	G	H	I
J	K	L	M	N	O	P	Q	R
S	T	U	V	W	X	Y	Z	

Miriam Roberts

Step 1

As shown in Mary Ann Smith's sample chart on the following page, write your year of birth across the page and include every year, up to and including the year you wish to calculate your Essence Number for. For example, if you were born in 1969 and wish to know your Essence Numbers up to the year 2017, you need to write every year from 1969 to 2017. Sorry, but there's no shortcut in this calculation, and you can't just fast-forward to 2017. You have to begin at the birth year.

Step 2

As shown in the sample chart below, place your age underneath the relevant year starting from year 0 up to the age you wish to calculate your Essence Number for. For the sake of the example, we'll calculate up to age 22 in 1991.

Please note: *Some numerologists begin the Table of Events chart at age 1, and some begin with age 0 (which covers the months from birth to age 1). It's up to you which age you prefer to begin with. Personally, I begin with 0.*

Sample Table of Events Chart for Mary Ann Smith (12-11-1969)																						
Year																						
69	70	71	72	73	74	75	76	77	78	79	80	81	82	83	84	85	86	87	88	89	90	91
Age																						
0	1	2	3	4	5	6	7	8	9	10	11	12	13	14	15	16	17	18	19	20	21	22

Step 3

Using the sample chart on the following page, place your relevant Physical Transit Number under its corresponding year and age. Remember, your Physical Transit Numbers are the letters in your first name, and the duration of each Transit varies depending on the numerical value of the letter. (See the Western letters-and-numbers chart for the numerical value of each letter.)

For example, in the name Mary Ann Smith, we use *MARY* to calculate the Physical Transit Numbers because it's the first name. We begin by placing the first letter, *M,* which has a numerical value of 4, under the first year, 1969, and age 0 on the Table of Events. Next, we place the second *M* under the second year, 1970, and age 1. The third *M* goes under 1971 and age 2, and the fourth *M* goes under 1972 and age 3, until we get to the next Transit letter in the name, which is *A*. Because *A* has a numerical value of 1, it is only used once, under 1973 and age 4.

Now we move on to the next Transit letter, *R,* which has a numerical value of 9. Therefore, *R* is placed under the years 1974 to 1982 and the ages 5 to 13. The final Transit letter, *Y,* with a numerical value of 7, is placed under years 1983 to 1989 and ages 14 to 20.

Once you've worked your way through every Transit letter in the name, you then repeat the process again up to the year/age you wish to calculate the Essence Number for. (If you happen to have a hyphenated first name, it is written as one name.)

Sample Table of Events Chart for Mary Ann Smith (12-11-1969)																						
Year																						
69	70	71	72	73	74	75	76	77	78	79	80	81	82	83	84	85	86	87	88	89	90	91
Age																						
0	1	2	3	4	5	6	7	8	9	10	11	12	13	14	15	16	17	18	19	20	21	22
Physical Transit (First Name)																						
M	M	M	M	A	R	R	R	R	R	R	R	R	R	Y	Y	Y	Y	Y	Y	Y	M	M

Step 4

Once again, the same process is used for the Mental Transit, as seen in the sample chart that follows. Place your relevant Mental

Transit Number under its corresponding year, age, and Physical Transit Number. Remember, your Mental Transit Numbers are the letters in your middle name, and the duration of each Transit varies depending on the numerical value of the letter. If you don't have a middle name, you can skip this step. If you have several middle names, they are written as one name.

For example, in the name Mary Ann Smith, we use *ANN* to calculate the Mental Transit Numbers because it's the middle name. We begin by placing the first letter, *A*, which has a numerical value of 1, under the first birth year, 1969, and age 0. Next, we place the second letter, *N*, with a numerical value of 5, under years 1970 to 1974 and ages 1 to 5. The final letter is another *N*, also with a numerical value of 5, and it goes under years 1975 to 1979 and ages 6 to 10. We then repeat the process until the year/age we wish to calculate the Essence Number for.

Sample Table of Events Chart for Mary Ann Smith (12-11-1969)																						
Year																						
69	70	71	72	73	74	75	76	77	78	79	80	81	82	83	84	85	86	87	88	89	90	91
Age																						
0	1	2	3	4	5	6	7	8	9	10	11	12	13	14	15	16	17	18	19	20	21	22
Physical Transit (First Name)																						
M	M	M	M	A	R	R	R	R	R	R	R	R	R	Y	Y	Y	Y	Y	Y	Y	M	M
Mental Transit (Middle Name)																						
A	N	N	N	N	N	N	N	N	N	N	A	N	N	N	N	N	N	N	N	N	N	A

Step 5

Once again, the same process is used for the Spiritual Transit, as shown in the sample chart that follows. Place your relevant Spiritual Transit Number under its corresponding year, age, and Physical and Mental Transit Numbers. Remember, your Spiritual Transit Numbers are the letters in your last name, and the duration of each

Transit varies depending on the numerical value of the letter. If you have a hyphenated surname, it is written as one name.

For example, in the name Mary Ann Smith, we use *SMITH* to calculate the Spiritual Transit Numbers because it's the last name. We begin by placing the first letter, *S,* which has a numerical value of 1, under the first birth year, 1969, and age 0. Next, we place the second letter, *M,* with a numerical value of 4, under 1970 to 1973 and ages 1 to 4. The next letter, *I,* with a numerical value of 9, goes under years 1974 to 1982 and ages 6 to 13. *T* comes next, with a numerical value of 2, and goes under 1983 to 1984 and ages 14 to 15. The final letter, *H,* with a numerical value of 8, goes under 1985 and age 16 and continues on until the end of our sample chart. Once all of your Transit letters have been calculated, repeat the process until the year/age you wish to calculate the Essence Number for.

Sample Table of Events Chart for Mary Ann Smith (12-11-1969)

Year																						
69	70	71	72	73	74	75	76	77	78	79	80	81	82	83	84	85	86	87	88	89	90	91
Age																						
0	1	2	3	4	5	6	7	8	9	10	11	12	13	14	15	16	17	18	19	20	21	22
Physical Transit (First Name)																						
M	M	M	M	A	R	R	R	R	R	R	R	R	R	Y	Y	Y	Y	Y	Y	Y	M	M
Mental Transit (Middle Name)																						
A	N	N	N	N	N	N	N	N	N	N	A	N	N	N	N	N	N	N	N	N	N	A
Spiritual Transit (Surname)																						
S	M	M	M	M	I	I	I	I	I	I	I	I	I	T	T	H	H	H	H	H	H	H

Now let's calculate the Essence Numbers.

How to Calculate Your Essence Numbers

The Essence Number is calculated by adding all the Transit letters together for a particular age and year.

Step 1

Using the Western letters-and-numbers chart, total the Physical, Mental, and Spiritual Transit Numbers together to calculate your Essence Number. Be mindful of any double-digit compound numbers before reducing down to a single-digit Essence Number.

Please note: *Karmic Debt Numbers 13/4, 14/5, 16/7, and 19/1 and Master Numbers 11/2 and 22/4 also apply to Essence Numbers and are written as 13/4, 14/5, 16/7, 19/1, 11/2, and 22/4.*

1	2	3	4	5	6	7	8	9
A	B	C	D	E	F	G	H	I
J	K	L	M	N	O	P	Q	R
S	T	U	V	W	X	Y	Z	

Miriam Roberts

As in Mary Ann Smith's sample chart below, from birth (age 0) until the age of 1, Mary had a 6 Essence Number because *M* (4) + *A* (1) + *S* (1) = 6. At age 1 she had a 13/4 Essence Number because *M* (4) + *N* (5) + *M* (4) = 13, which is written as 13/4 because it's a Karmic Debt Number and doesn't reduce down to a 4. Because Mary had that same sequence of Transits until the age of 4, she remained in a 13/4 Essence Number for three years. At age 4, the

Transit sequence changed to a 1 Essence Number because *A* (1) + *N* (5) + *M* (4) = 10, which reduces down to a 1. Then the Transit sequence changed once more at age 5 to a 5 Essence Number because *R* (9) + *N* (5) + *I* (9) = 23, which reduces down to a 5. And the process continues on like so until you arrive at the year/age you wish to calculate the Essence Number for.

Step 2

For additional insight and information, write the Personal Year Number for each corresponding year and age underneath the Essence Number on the Table of Events chart. That way, the Essence Number, Personal Year Number, and individual Transits can provide the overall picture of what is influencing your life during the course of a particular year.

Sample Table of Events Chart for Mary Ann Smith (12-11-1969)																						
Year																						
69	70	71	72	73	74	75	76	77	78	79	80	81	82	83	84	85	86	87	88	89	90	91
Age																						
0	1	2	3	4	5	6	7	8	9	10	11	12	13	14	15	16	17	18	19	20	21	22
Physical Transit (First Name)																						
M	M	M	M	A	R	R	R	R	R	R	R	R	R	R	Y	Y	Y	Y	Y	Y	M	M
Mental Transit (Middle Name)																						
A	N	N	N	N	N	N	N	N	N	N	A	N	N	N	N	N	N	N	N	N	N	A
Spiritual Transit (Surname)																						
S	M	M	M	M	I	I	I	I	I	I	I	I	I	I	T	T	H	H	H	H	H	H
Essence Number (Transit Total)																						
6	13	13	13	10	23	23	23	23	23	23	19	23	23	14	14	20	20	20	20	20	17	13
	4	4	4	1	5	5	5	5	5	5	1	5	5	5	5	2	2	2	2	2	8	4
Personal Year																						
3	4	5	6	7	8	9	1	2	3	4	5	6	7	8	9	1	2	3	4	5	6	7

The Essence Number is the key to deeper understanding and awareness, especially when it comes to the circumstances surrounding your Personal Year Number. For example, if you're in a 1 Personal Year of new beginnings with a 4 or 13/4 Essence Number, you know in advance that extra effort is required to create a fresh start. Due to the influence of the 4, you'll know you'll need to work hard to achieve your desired results. So you can adopt a positive mind-set, focus on achieving your goals, and prepare to persevere. On the other hand, if you had a 1 Essence with your 1 Personal Year, you'd know you have a double green light to move forward and that new beginnings and opportunities will present themselves with greater ease.

✴

If you managed to calculate your Essence Numbers and assemble a Table of Events chart, give yourself a massive pat on the back, because that's a very big achievement! The Essence Number is by far the most challenging number to calculate in a numerology chart. It's so challenging, in fact, that many numerologists leave it out of their teachings altogether! However, you cannot give an accurate forecast without this vital piece of information.

Now that you've seen how much work is involved in calculating your numbers manually, you can understand why so many numerologists (including me) use numerology software to calculate their charts. Numerology software can be purchased through various websites; however, I recommend you view as many sample reports and download as many free software trials as you can before making a purchase. Also, be sure that the software you purchase includes the Essence Number, as some programs don't.

Because *a number has the same meaning wherever it appears*, I suggest that you read the Karmic Debt, Personal Year, Major Life Cycle, Challenge, and Pinnacle Number descriptions for additional insight into the Essence Number meanings. With that being said, let's take a look at the Essence Number meanings.

Essence Number Meanings

1 Essence Number

During a 1 Essence, you'll want to create a fresh start and experience new things, and there will be many opportunities to do so. You will have numerous creative and innovative ideas and the motivation to bring them to fruition, but you must remain confident and strong. You'll feel a need to break free from restrictions and gain your independence, especially if you're feeling disempowered or repressed. This is a time to embrace your individuality and have the courage to stand up for yourself. You may also feel a desire to become a leader in your field.

2 Essence Number

During a 2 Essence, you'll feel a need to form deep and meaningful connections with others, and your relationships will take center stage. Relationship issues will arise in order to be worked through, and in some cases, a relationship may end; however, this is also a time where new partnerships and romances can *begin.* Your heightened sense of awareness enables you to perceive others' needs so you can cooperate more effectively. Due to your enhanced sensitivity and intuition, there's a need to balance your emotions and remain grounded at all times. Unresolved emotional issues may surface to be processed once and for all. This is a time of slow development requiring patience.

3 Essence Number

During a 3 Essence, you'll find yourself drawn to creative endeavors and will have a knack for expressing yourself with your words, body movements, intellect, or hands. Whether it's writing, decorating, photography, designing, painting, dancing, cooking,

185

or gardening, any form of creative expression is favored during this time. This is also a period of heightened emotions, and whether they're positive or negative depends on where you focus your attention. This is a time of fun, friendship, and laughter, where unresolved emotions will surface to be dealt with.

4 Essence Number

During a 4 Essence, you'll feel the need to settle down and take your responsibilities seriously. Whether this relates to your finances, relationships, home life, or career, you'll feel a need to improve your environment and stabilize your life. This cycle requires dedication, effort, and hard work. Despite your feelings of limitation and restriction, with discipline, focus, and determination, you can achieve your goals. Your mind-set is the key to making the most of this cycle. Patience, persistence, and positivity will help you achieve your desired results.

5 Essence Number

During a 5 Essence, you'll want to break free from responsibility and restriction and add some adventure to your life. This is a time of progress, movement, and change as you seek to explore new people, places, and life experiences. Using your freedom constructively is the key to your success during this highly dynamic time, as is remaining focused and grounded. Be mindful not to overindulge in things that pleasure the senses—*moderation* is essential. Travel and communication endeavors are favored, and there will be many opportunities for growth and expansion. Be flexible and adaptable to change . . . and expect the unexpected.

6 Essence Number

During a 6 Essence, you'll feel the need to focus on your relationships, family, and home. Love takes center stage as any unresolved relationship issues surface to be addressed. You'll feel a need for romance and partnership, and if you're looking for love, opportunities will present themselves. There's a great need to balance your home life with your career, as you may be called upon to assist loved ones in need. This is a favorable time to give birth, raise children, and build upon an existing love relationship. It's also the ideal time to leave an unhealthy relationship behind. Your creative abilities are enhanced, as is your ability to give and receive love, but you must define your personal boundaries and balance others' needs with your own.

7 Essence Number

During a 7 Essence, you'll feel the need to spend quiet time alone in contemplation and self-reflection. This is a time to go within rather than take the world by storm. You may find yourself defending your need to be alone to those who take it as a personal rejection of their company. This is the perfect opportunity to read, teach, study, or specialize within your craft. Since this is a time of spiritual awakening, you may find yourself drawn to spirituality and alternative therapies and teachings. Health and personal development come to the forefront as you question yourself, your future, and the overall meaning of life. This is a time to focus on yourself and improving your quality of life. Meditation and prayer are extremely beneficial during this pivotal time.

8 Essence Number

During an 8 Essence, you'll feel the need to take care of business as your finances and career take center stage. Your professional reputation also comes to the fore as opportunities for rewards and recognition present themselves. This is also a test of your integrity and underlying motivations, so be honest, hardworking, appreciative, and generous at all times in order to reap the fruits of your labor. It is vital that you adopt an attitude of abundance during this cycle and keep your finances in order. You may feel the need to reclaim your personal power by confronting anyone or anything that has taken your power away. This is a powerful Essence of manifestation to actualize your dreams.

9 Essence Number

During a 9 Essence, you'll feel a need to let go of the past and move toward better things. Forgiveness is essential to your transformation and well-being during this time, as is your need to remove anything from your life that no longer serves your greater good. This can be a challenging time if you fear change or the unknown; however, there is much potential for success when you have the courage to move on. Your creative abilities are enhanced during this cycle, and you are being encouraged to serve, comfort, and heal those in need. You may feel drawn to humanitarian or environmental causes during this period of endings and completion.

MASTER NUMBER ESSENCE NUMBERS

Master Numbers 11/2 and 22/4 are high-potency Essence Numbers that bring extra opportunities for growth, illumination, and transformation. I suggest you read the 11/2 and 22/4 Personal Year Number meanings for added insight into these numbers.

11/2 Essence Number

Also read the description for 2 Essence Number.

During an 11/2 Essence, you'll experience everything that falls under the 2 Essence, along with a greater depth of understanding and awareness of yourself and the world around you. This is a time of personal transformation and spiritual awakening as you question the meaning of life. Your enhanced intuition enables you to make better decisions that stem from a deep inner knowing; however, your heightened sensitivity may cause you to feel self-protective and insecure. This is a pivotal time in your development that will enhance your connection to the Divine (God/Universe/Source). So maintain a positive mind-set, spend time in nature, meditate, pray, and create a harmonious environment around you to make the most of this cycle.

22/4 Essence Number

Also read the description for 4 Essence Number.

During a 22/4 Essence, you'll experience everything that falls under the 4 Essence, along with added potential for recognition and accomplishment. During this cycle, you have the ability to manifest ideas into physical form through practical action, discipline, and a higher awareness. Your commitment and integrity will be tested, but if you live by your higher ideals, the opportunities are endless. This is a time requiring strength, dedication, and effort, where you'll be encouraged to serve the greater good. This Essence provides the opportunity to implement, manage, or support a large-scale endeavor that serves the community or humanity as a whole, with much potential for success.

KARMIC DEBT ESSENCE NUMBERS

Karmic Debt Numbers 13/4, 14/5, 16/7, and 19/1 are high-potency Essence Numbers that bring extra challenges and opportunities for growth. I suggest you read the Karmic Debt Number meanings in Part I for added insight into these numbers.

13/4 Essence Number

Also read the description for 4 Essence Number.

During a 13/4 Essence, you'll experience everything that falls under the 4 Essence, along with an added sense of frustration due to your inability to achieve your desired outcomes and results. Your lesson during this time is to put extra effort into your projects and avoid the temptation to manipulate a situation or take the easy way out. Honesty, integrity, perseverance, and patience are the keys to your success.

14/5 Essence Number

Also read the description for 5 Essence Number.

During a 14/5 Essence, you'll experience everything that falls under the 5 Essence, along with an added need to display temperance and moderation at all times. Despite how enticing the opportunities may be, you must rise above your earthly desires during this highly addictive cycle. Your lesson is to remain grounded, centered, disciplined, and responsible during this Essence of temptation.

16/7 Essence Number

Also read the description for 7 Essence Number.

During a 16/7 Essence, you'll experience everything that falls under the 7 Essence, along with an added need to trust and surrender to the challenging or unexpected events in your life. To make the most of this cycle, you must let go of the past, rise above your ego and any superficial tendencies, and have faith in the Divine plan of your life. You must also be honest in love and treat others with respect. At the conclusion of this Essence, you'll be wiser, stronger, and personally transformed.

19/1 Essence Number

Also read the description for 1 Essence Number.

During a 19/1 Essence, you'll experience everything that falls under the 1 Essence, along with an added sense of frustration due to your inability to control your environment and/or the people in your life. Your lesson during this time is to take others' needs and opinions into consideration rather than just your own and to accept assistance from others. By having the courage to admit your mistakes and overcome your pride, you'll conclude this Essence with added wisdom and compassion.

✦ ✦ ✦

Blending Everything Together

Now that you're familiar with the 7 Core Numbers and numerology cycles, the key to a thorough and accurate reading lies in blending everything together. This requires as much *common sense* and *logic* as it does *intuition* and *insight*. You must use both your instincts and your reasoning to see the overall picture and put everything together. Here are a few tips and reminders to get you started:

— There's a positive and negative expression of every number; therefore, you must determine whether a person is expressing the positive or negative aspect of his or her numbers to give an accurate interpretation.

— For greater accuracy in personality profiling, be mindful of opposing Core Numbers that create balance. For example, a 4 or 7 Life Path with a 3 or 5 among the 7 Core Numbers is going to be more social, creative, and outgoing than a 4 or 7 without these. This also applies to the presence of a 3 or 5 in a double-digit compound number prior to reducing down to a single-digit number—that is,

31/4 or 34/7. Also, due to the double presence of the sensitive 2s, a 22/4 is more sensitive and emotional than other 4s.

Alternatively, a 3 or 5 Life Path who has a 4, 6, or 8 among the 7 Core Numbers is going to be more grounded, responsible, and consistent than a 3 or 5 who doesn't. This also applies to the presence of a 4, 6, or 8 in a double-digit compound number prior to reducing down to a single-digit number—that is, 48/12/3, 41/5, or 14/5.

— Be mindful of conflicting numbers and cycles. For example, when a 5 Life Path (the Freedom-Loving Adventurer) is in a 6 cycle of responsibility and commitment or a 4 cycle of stability and limitation, it can cause a feeling of frustration due to the intrinsic desire to be unrestricted and free. Use your common sense to determine where possible conflicts could occur.

— If you're in the same Major Life Cycle, Pinnacle, or Personal Year Number as one of your 7 Core Numbers—especially the Life Path or Destiny Number—the cycle energy is enhanced. Additional opportunities to fulfill your destiny will present themselves during the course of that cycle.

— Evaluate a cycle in relation to the Life Path Number for added insight. For example, if a positive 8 Life Path (the Business-Minded Leader) is in an 8 cycle (a cycle of business and career), it's highly probable he or she will start a business, get a promotion, or rise to a position of authority during that cycle. A 7 Life Path (the Contemplative Truth Seeker) is more likely to want company and form meaningful connections with others in a 2, 3, or 6 cycle.

— Review the 7 Core Numbers in relation to the Personal Year and Essence Numbers for added insight. For example, somebody who has a 5 among his or her 7 Core Numbers is more likely to throw caution to the wind in a 5 Essence or Personal Year than somebody with a responsible 4 or 6.

— Focus predominantly on the Essence and Personal Year Numbers for a yearly forecast, as they have the most dominant influence over the circumstances of the year.

— The circumstances of a cycle number can be experienced at any time in a person's life. For example, you don't have to be in a 2 or 6 cycle to experience love or in an 8 cycle to focus on your finances and career. These circumstances can be experienced during any cycle. The cycle numbers mean that there will be a greater emphasis on these circumstances during that particular cycle.

As you can imagine, there are countless other things to take into consideration to give an accurate reading, and it's impossible to list them all. But as you grow to be more familiar with numerology, you'll come to some logical conclusions of your own. As long as you aim to see the bigger picture and take everything into account, you'll provide a thorough interpretation and do a fantastic job!

+ + +

PART III

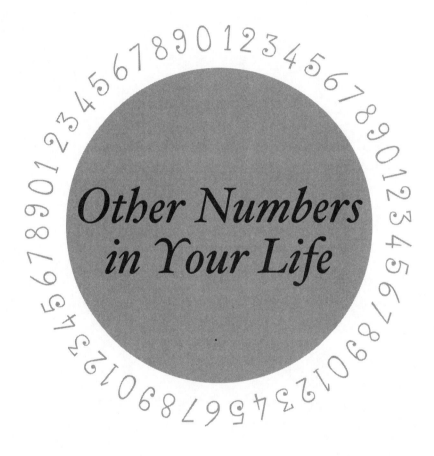

Other Numbers in Your Life

What's in a Name?

Phew! Now that the hard stuff is out of the way, let's take a look at some of the other numbers in your life, starting with those pertaining to your name.

CHANGING A NAME

Whether you know it or not, your name sends an energetic message to the world, so when you change your name, you change the content of your message. Any numerologist will tell you that a name change is a serious matter and that there are several things to take into consideration before you alter the course of your life.

Even though Western numerologists believe that the Destiny Number (calculated from your original birth-certificate name) has the greatest impact on your life, the first and last name you use on a daily basis (Current Name Number) brings additional talents, opportunities, life lessons, and challenges to the mix that combine with your existing Destiny Number. Your current first and last name also brings additional life experiences that may or may not assist you in fulfilling your prechosen destiny. Therefore, it's important to understand the nature of the number you're inheriting *before* you change your name.

By investigating the energy of your new name number in advance, you can determine whether it will help you fulfill your destiny and reach your full potential. You can examine whether your inherited personality traits, strengths, and opportunities will assist you in accomplishing your hopes and dreams. You can also determine whether you're up for the extra lessons and challenges.

Be aware that changing your name will not eliminate or help you avoid the life lessons from your original birth-certificate name, because the energy of that name remains with you for life. You've prechosen those particular lessons for the evolution of your soul, and they'll continue to appear in your life until you master them once and for all. On the other hand, a name change can enhance or dimimish your ability to overcome those lessons, depending on how your new name number relates to your existing numbers. In other words, there's no point in changing your name in the hopes of escaping your current life and the past.

Besides, every number has lessons and challenges. Some people prefer to stick with the name they have so they can master the numbers they're already working with. They believe that adding a new energy to the mix isn't worth the trouble. In most cases, though, women change their name as a result of marriage without giving it a second thought.

Examine Your Motivation

If you're thinking of changing your name, it's important to examine your motivation. If it's due to a transition such as marriage or divorce, or a career necessity, then your reason is legitimate and in harmony with the natural flow of life. Other valid reasons may be a wish to have the same surname as your children, wanting to change to a name that's easier for others to spell or pronounce, or the desire to release a last name due to an abusive past experience.

Motivations such as these are logical no-brainers, but when the motivation is self-gain, it can be more trouble than it's worth. Illegal or ego-driven motivations such as avoiding the taxman, escaping a dodgy past, or hoping to become rich and famous can create negative karma and have the *opposite* of the desired effect. So dig deep and be honest with yourself when determining your underlying motivation for changing your name, and make sure your intentions align with your higher ideals and serve your greater good. And most of all, remember that only *you* can create a better life for yourself, not your name. Only your own thoughts, beliefs, and actions can improve the circumstances of your life.

Choosing a Name

When choosing a name, before you even begin to work out the numbers, you must go by how you *feel*. This is because your intuition (which is the voice of your soul) knows the perfect name to carry you through the next phase of your life. Before you dig out your "numerology" calculator, spend some quiet time alone meditating on your new name to examine whether it looks, sounds, and feels as if it fits.

The reason why your intuition is so important when choosing a name is because only your soul (rather than your ego mind) knows the perfect name to help you reach your full potential. Only your soul knows the ideal name to help you overcome your future challenges and utilize the opportunities coming your way. Your soul will make this name known to you by having it *feel* like it fits or by sending you a sign. So pay attention to your feelings, and be on the lookout for confirmation of a name you're considering. Remember to pray and ask your higher self, spirit guides, angels, and God (Universe/the Divine) for assistance in deciding.

The trouble with calculating a name number prior to making your decision is that once the ego mind gets involved, your intuition goes out the window. Once you calculate the numbers, you may decide to choose a name with the most "glamorous" number or with the number you think will provide the easiest life. As challenging as it may be, you need to stick to your guns and base your decision on intuition, because the name that *feels* best will provide the best life in the end.

If you have several names that feel right and wish to investigate the numbers, or if you don't give a hoot about intuition and *only* care about the numbers, here are some valuable tips.

Tips for Choosing a Name

- Determine whether your new name number will support you in fulfilling your destiny.

- Choose a name number that is compatible with the existing Core Numbers in your chart—especially the Life Path, Destiny, Soul, and Maturity Numbers. A name that is compatible with your original birth-certificate name (Destiny Number) can work to your advantage by emphasizing the existing energy you've already chosen to master.

- Consider a name number that's the same as your Life Path, Destiny, Soul, or Maturity Number to enhance that existing energy. Or, on the other hand, consider choosing a name number that you're missing in your 7 Core Numbers to attain balance and self-mastery.

- Establish where you may be out of balance in your chart, and consider a name number that can even things out. For example, a chart with several 3s or 5s would benefit from the grounding energy of 4 or 8. This is an example where opposite numbers can work to your advantage.

- Avoid Karmic Debt Numbers 13/4, 14/5, 16/7, or 19/1 unless you're up for the extra challenge!

- Avoid a name number already contained in your chart two or more times. Excess energy can reveal the challenging aspect of that number.

- If you choose a name number totaling a Master Number 11/2, 22/4, or 33/6, make sure you're prepared for additional trials and tribulations on your journey to self-mastery.

- Choose a name number with the qualities you'd like to activate and enhance within yourself. To view some of those qualities, read the Current Name Number description, along with every other description for that number.

When to Change Your Name

Changing your name during a favorable cycle can be beneficial but isn't essential; however, if you're in a position to wait, why not hold out until you're in a 1 cycle of new beginnings or a 5 cycle of change? By changing your name under a natural vibration of change, or embarking upon a new beginning under a natural vibration of new beginnings, you can "birth" your new name into the world harmoniously. On the other hand, if holding out until you're in a 1 or 5 Personal Year is too long to wait, why not consider a 1 or 5 Personal Month or Personal Day? If none of these options are possible, it's not the end of the world. You can experience a harmonious name-change transition with the power of belief.

Activating Your New Name Energy

It can take between five to nine years (a full Personal Year Cycle) for a new name energy to take full effect; however, subtle changes can be felt as soon as you begin to use the name. The degree of influence your new name will have upon your life is determined by how often it's used. For it to have a significant impact, it must be fully embraced and used on a daily basis. You will also need to identify and resonate emotionally with your new name in order to activate its vibration and attract its energy into your life.

If you want to activate your new name energy sooner, you're going to need to "walk the talk" and "fake it 'til you make it" by adopting the tendencies of the number. For example, if you're inheriting a 3 name to enhance your creative abilities, you'll need to spend more time being creative in your everyday life. You'll also need to persevere at mastering your craft; you can't expect the number to do everything for you! You have to meet the Universe halfway and put the effort in yourself.

To activate your new name energy, you're also going to need to take physical action by changing your signature and renaming your bank account, club memberships, e-mail address, credit cards, power- and telephone-company account holders, Facebook and Twitter accounts, and so on . . . as well as reprinting your business cards and making every other necessary change that will enforce your new name. Don't forget that you'll need to make it legal and official by changing your passport and driver's license and updating your details with the appropriate government departments. And remember: the greater attention you give your new name, the more you strengthen its vibration. So insist that your friends, family, work colleagues, and acquaintances address you by your new name at all times.

Maiden or Married Name After Marriage?

Deciding whether to take your husband's name after marriage is a no-brainer for many; however, more and more women these days prefer to keep their maiden names for personal or professional reasons. Only *you* can determine what's best for you, and there's no right or wrong answer. Just be sure you base your decision on your intuition, rather than your rational mind.

If your maiden name happens to be your original birth-certificate name (Destiny Number), its energy remains with you throughout the course of your life. It contains the ancestral blueprint of your family and can never be replaced. When you change your last name through marriage, you inherit your husband's ancestral blueprint, also, and all of the energetic qualities that go with it. If you choose to take your husband's name, check out the name number qualities you'll inherit—and enhance within yourself—by calculating your Current Name Number. Remember, when you change your name, you change your energy vibration, and some women actually turn into a different person after marriage. (Fingers crossed that the new person you become is still a vibrational match with your hubby!)

For those who choose to use a hyphenated last name, consider the surname *one* name when calculating the numbers. Regardless of what you decide, be sure you make your decision for *yourself,* rather than to please others. You're the one who has to live under the new vibration, after all.

Married, Maiden, or New Name After Divorce?

After a divorce, you can decide whether to keep your married name, revert back to your maiden name, or create a new name altogether. Once again, there's no right or wrong. It simply comes down to personal preference and, of course, whatever *feels* right to you.

When deciding whether or not to keep your married name, you must try to keep your personal feelings regarding your ex-husband and your marriage out of the decision. Strangely enough, despite a failed marriage, you'd be surprised how often your married name can continue to serve you in your life. Even though the marriage itself didn't work out, in some cases your married name can still help you reach your full potential. If you follow your intuition and investigate the energy of the number, you'll be able to determine whether it can assist you on your path.

On the other hand, you may have outgrown the need to include this name energy on your journey and may have learned everything you needed to learn from this number and experience. When this is the case, there will be no doubt in your heart and mind that it's time to kick your married name to the curb and revert back to your maiden name—or use a new name. Keep in mind that it takes between five to nine years for your married name to fully integrate into your life, so if you divorce within that time, the transition back to your maiden name will be relatively minor.

Remember, your first and last name sends an energetic message to the world, and when you change your name, you change the content of your message. So you don't want to change your name willy-nilly. Take your time deciding and listen to your heart.

CHOOSING A PET'S NAME

Your pet's name also sends an energetic message to the world and influences its behavior. That said, choosing a name for your pet is a lot less involved than choosing a name for a baby (as you'll discover in the "Choosing a Baby's Name" section to come). However, one thing's for certain: when naming a pet—yep, you guessed it—you must listen to your intuition first! Always go with the name that *feels* right before you start working out the numbers. Then, when you've decided on a name, you can investigate the numbers to see what you can expect from your little (or not-so-little) animal friend.

When choosing a name for a cat or dog, one- and two-syllable words tend to work best. It also pays to take the harmonics of the name into consideration by determining how it falls on the ears. Does it have a pleasant sound, or does something not sound or feel right? Does it feel like it fits? You might try using the name for a few days to observe your pet's response before making your final decision.

How about taking your pet's Life Path Number into consideration when making your decision? You may end up choosing a name that balances its energy and harmonizes with your own. Use the Life Path Number calculation formula in Part I to calculate your pet's Life Path Number, and use your common sense to apply the Life Path Number meanings to your pet.

How to Calculate a Pet Name Number

A Pet Name Number is calculated using the exact same formula to calculate the Destiny Number for a person; however, you don't need to include your family's last name. Why not calculate the Soul and Personality Numbers while you're at it for additional information?

Now let's take a look at the Pet Name Number meanings to give you an idea of what you can expect from your furry, feathered, or finned friend:

Pet Name Number Meanings

1 Pet Name Number

This animal is independent, strong-minded, and can take care of itself. This is a great name number for a pet that may need to spend a lot of time alone. This animal really likes to be #1 and tends to rule the roost, so it may not harmonize easily with other pets unless it gets to be the boss.

2 Pet Name Number

This animal is sensitive, loving, and affectionate. This is a great name number for a pet you want to snuggle up with and who will comfort you when you're down. Number 2 pets need company, along with a peaceful and harmonious environment; otherwise, they can act out or become unwell.

3 Pet Name Number

This animal is extremely playful and likes to have fun. This is a great name number for a pet who will socialize with people and other animals. Number 3 pets need regular stimulation, activity, and entertainment. They're lovable and friendly but can be hyperactive and cheeky.

4 Pet Name Number

This animal is loyal, reliable, and fairly easy to train. This is a great name number for a pet that doesn't require your constant affection and attention. Security, stability, and routine make number 4 pets happy, so if you tend to move around a lot, you might consider another name.

5 Pet Name Number

This animal is adventurous and needs plenty of exercise and stimulation. This is a great name number for a pet that has a lot of space and freedom to explore. Very social, number 5 pets need other animals for company. If they feel lonely or bored, they can be troublesome and naughty.

6 Pet Name Number

This animal is affectionate and loves to be part of the family. This is a great name number for a pet that can grow up alongside children. Very caring and protective, number 6 pets will defend you at all costs, but if they have to share your attention, they can be jealous and possessive.

7 Pet Name Number

This animal enjoys its own company and can entertain itself. This is a great name number for a pet that needs to spend a lot of time alone. Intelligent and observant, number 7 pets like to watch what's going on. Strangers may need to earn their trust, but they'll be loyal to the bitter end.

8 Pet Name Number

This animal is regal, majestic, and the leader of the pack. This is a great name number for a show animal or a pet that is highly focused on appearance. Number 8 pets are independent and strong and like to be the kings of the castle, so if you treat this animal like royalty, you'll have a loving friend for life.

9 Pet Name Number

This animal is sensitive, wise, and intense. This is a great name number for a family pet who grows up around children. A number 9 pet is very in tune with its surroundings and will know when something's wrong. As long as this animal feels included, it will never let you down.

11/2 Pet Name Number

Also read the description for 2 Pet Name Number.

This animal is extremely sensitive and intuitive. This is a great name number for a pet you'd like to accompany you on your journey toward enlightenment. Pets who are 11/2s are very deep and loving but can be jealous and obsessive, too. They can be hypersensitive to food additives, as well as negative energy and environments. They may prefer company over being alone.

22/4 Pet Name Number

Also read the description for 4 Pet Name Number.

This animal is extremely devoted and eager to please. This is a great name number for a pet you want to be your best friend. Protective and loyal, 22/4 pets make good guard dogs. They're fairly easy to train, but due to the Master Number vibration, they can be hypersensitive to food additives, as well as negative energy and environments.

33/6 Pet Name Number

Also read the description for 6 Pet Name Number.

This animal is extremely fun loving and affectionate. This is a great name number for a pet whose main role is to open your heart to love, as 33/6 pets are natural caregivers and healers. This is the ideal name for a pet who will provide companionship and fun. Due to the Master Number vibration, 33/6 pets can be hypersensitive to food additives, as well as negative energy and environments.

CHOOSING A BUSINESS NAME

The key to choosing a good business name is to pick one that will help your business thrive and allow you to achieve your goals. Therefore, the very first step is to determine what those goals are by asking the question: *What do I hope to accomplish with this business?*

All business owners want their companies to be successful and profitable (8); therefore, that particular goal is a no-brainer. However, you'll also need to look outside of your financial aspirations to clarify other business goals you may hope to achieve. For example, you may want your business to serve the community (6, 9) and be innovative and pioneering (1, 5).

Next, you'll need to pinpoint your business's talents and abilities in order to find the numbers that will enhance those natural energies. For example, a web-design company's talents and abilities are creativity and communication; therefore, a 3 Business Name Number representing these traits would enhance its creative ideas, along with its ability to communicate them.

It's helpful, but not essential, to find a Business Name Number that harmonizes with your Life Path, Destiny, or Soul Number—especially if you're a sole proprietor. But don't worry if this isn't possible. The main consideration is to find a business name that accentuates the natural energy of the business, which will help it achieve its goals.

How to Calculate a Business Name Number

A Business Name Number is calculated using the exact same formula to calculate a person's Destiny Number.

Step 1

Use the Western letters-and-numbers chart below to match the corresponding numbers to the letters in your business name. Be sure to use the name that appears on your signage, promotional materials, and business card. Feel free to use whichever method you choose to calculate your Business Name Number. Let's use the reducing-down method as an example.

1	2	3	4	5	6	7	8	9
A	B	C	D	E	F	G	H	I
J	K	L	M	N	O	P	Q	R
S	T	U	V	W	X	Y	Z	

Miriam Roberts

Step 2

Add each word separately to create individual totals, then reduce each total down to single-digit numbers.

Please note: *Whether you reduce numbers 11, 22, or 33 down to 2, 4, or 6 at this stage of the calculation is up to you.*

211

Step 3

Add all single numbers together and reduce them down to get a single-digit Business Name Number, unless they total 11, 22, or 33, which then becomes an 11/2, 22/4, or 33/6 Business Name Number. Let's use *PAWS AND CLAWS* as an example business name.

P A W S	A N D	C L A W S	
7+1+5+1	1+5+4	3+3+1+5+1	
14	10	13	
1+4	1+0	1+3	
5 +	1 +	4	= 10

1+0 = **1 Business Name Number**

Once you've calculated your Business Name Number, calculate the Soul (vowels) and Personality (consonants) Numbers as well. That way you will get the bigger picture of the overall energy of the name.

❊

Now let's take a look at the Business Name Number meanings.

Business Name Number Meanings

1 Business Name Number

A 1 Business Name Number promotes innovation, creativity, and a pioneering spirit. It can help a business to be a trendsetter, front-runner, and market leader, because number 1 likes to be . . . #1. This name also promotes independence, strength, and courage. A business that prides itself on being original and unique and is driven to get things done can thrive under this number.

2 Business Name Number

A 2 Business Name Number is ideal for a partnership, team-oriented business, or a company that focuses on details. It promotes harmony, cooperation, negotiation, and a peaceful resolution to conflict, so it's the ideal number for a law, mediation, or customer-service-focused business. Any business that specializes in food, nutrition, health, healing, counseling, music, creativity, or service can thrive under a 2 vibration.

3 Business Name Number

A 3 Business Name Number is ideal for a creative business of any kind, or one that specializes in communication or child care. It's also the perfect name number for actors; musicians; speakers; writers; producers; or any business endeavor involved in the literary, performing, or visual arts. Verbal and creative expression across the board can thrive under a 3 vibration. Whether you have a design, catering, culinary, beauty, hairstyling, apparel, graphic-design, photography, decorating, landscaping, or jewelry-making business, the opportunities are endless.

4 Business Name Number

A 4 Business Name Number is ideal for a business that promotes stability or builds, manages, or organizes—such as construction, architecture, accounting, life coaching, teaching, or de-cluttering. Anything to do with auditing, law, planning, banking, or finance can thrive under this vibration. It's also a good number for those working with land, such as farming, landscaping, gardening, or real estate.

5 Business Name Number

A 5 Business Name Number is perfect for a travel, communication, hospitality, sales, media, PR, marketing, consulting, or event-management business. Any endeavor related to teaching, coaching, reporting, researching, and informing can thrive under a 5 vibration. This is a great name if your business is unconventional or if you happen to be a risk taker wanting to break new ground or introduce new products, concepts, and ideas.

6 Business Name Number

A 6 Business Name Number is perfect for those working in child care, education, healing, coaching, counseling, law, or the food and beauty industries. It is also the ideal number for a creative business, especially one that specializes in decor, design, or apparel. A grounded and well-rounded energy, 6 is the ideal Business Name Number for a service-based entity that prides itself on customer care.

7 Business Name Number

A 7 Business Name Number will assist a business that needs to uncover the truth and get to the bottom of things. If you're a researcher, reporter, writer, teacher, scientist, detective, technician, auditor, or analyst, this is the ideal number for you. An IT business can also thrive under this vibration. Since 7 promotes spiritual and personal growth, it's the perfect number for those working in metaphysics, healing, or conventional or alternative health. A 7 Business Name Number will help you become a specialist in your craft.

8 Business Name Number

An 8 Business Name Number will enhance your business's ability to generate income and sales, provided that it is operated with an attitude of abundance. The ideal number for self-employment, 8 is the "money number." However, business owners (and everyone associated with the business) must have a positive relationship with money and display honesty and integrity at all times; otherwise, it could have the opposite effect. Banking, finance, property, legal, management, and corporate businesses can thrive under an 8 vibration. But be aware: 8 is also a karmic number that can attract challenging lessons and a reversal of fortune.

9 Business Name Number

A 9 Business Name Number is ideal for a charity or a community-driven business. Those working in education, health care, healing, social work, and the law can thrive under a 9 vibration. This is also the ideal number for a creative, artistic, or service-based business or one that's involved with the literary, visual, or performing arts. Many designers, artists, musicians, speakers, writers, and actors flourish under a 9 Business Name Number. Anything to do with selfless service and humanitarian pursuits is also suited to a 9.

11/2 Business Name Number

Also read the description for 2 Business Name Number.
Because 11/2 is a Master Number energy, an 11/2 Business Name Number is best suited to a business that raises consciousness and spiritual awareness in some way. Any business that focuses on healing, metaphysics, counseling, coaching, music, inspirational speaking, and teaching can thrive under the 11/2 vibration. Actors, musicians, filmmakers, producers, inventors, and electricians can also benefit from this vibration.

22/4 Business Name Number

Also read the description for 4 Business Name Number.
Because 22/4 is a Master Number energy, a 22/4 Business Name Number is better suited to a business that serves the greater good

215

in some way. Any business that is driven to build, create, or promote something that is of benefit to humanity or the community, or that specializes in manifesting ideas into physical form, can thrive under the 22/4 vibration.

33/6 Business Name Number

Also read the description for 6 Business Name Number.

Because 33/6 is a Master Number energy, a 33/6 Business Name Number is better suited to a business that is dedicated to being of service or that provides healing in some way. Any business that promotes happiness and well-being through food, beauty, creativity, communication, music, law, or the healing arts can thrive under the 33/6 vibration. If your business involves child care, teaching, performing, caregiving, or the arts, then a 33/6 Business Name Number is ideal.

Remember, you can use this process to calculate the name number for anything! Whether it's a band, movie or book title, marketing campaign, workshop, or even a product such as perfume—if it's got a name, why not calculate its numbers!

✦ ✦ ✦

Parenting
by the Numbers

As parents and caregivers, we've chosen one of the most important jobs in the world—to be the teachers and guardians of our future generation. It's a huge responsibility, and it can be difficult and overwhelming at times. However, when we fully understand our children and their prechosen agendas, it can improve our relationships immensely. When we know our children's destiny and life purpose, we can then play a valuable role in helping them achieve it.

CHOOSING A BABY NAME

I cannot stress enough that when choosing a name for your baby, you must leave the numbers out altogether and base your decision purely on intuition. Your baby's birth-certificate name reflects his or her prechosen destiny and what he or she needs to accomplish in this life. Therefore, only your baby's soul could possibly know its agenda.

Your unborn baby will communicate this information to you—through your intuition or a sign. For example, you may watch a TV program or movie and fall in love with a character's name in the story, or you may meet an adorable child at the local park and want to use his or her name. You may be drawn to a parent or grandparent's name and feel within your heart that it's the perfect one to choose. A family member or friend may even suggest the ideal name. Either way, you'll know the name to choose because it *feels* right.

Whether you choose the name before or after your baby is born is irrelevant, as long as you base your decision on *intuition* rather than the numbers. Numerologists have conflicting opinions about this, but I feel strongly on this point. There are others who feel that it's the duty of parents to have a hand in the destiny of their unborn children by basing this decision purely on the numbers. However, I believe in choosing a name through intuition and then exploring the numbers *afterward* in order to prepare for what's in store.

I'm a numerologist, and I live the majority of my life by the numbers, but I chose both of my children's names without investigating the numbers in advance. I chose the names that stood out and that felt the best to me because I knew that, regardless of the numbers, these were the destinies my children had chosen for themselves. I believed that it was my responsibility as a parent to honor their decisions without putting my two cents' worth in. I didn't feel it was my place to manipulate their life journeys based on my ego's assumption of what their "ideal" numbers would be. As tempting as it was, I wasn't going to disrupt the natural flow of life.

Let me give you a real-life example of the effects outside interference can have in choosing a baby's name:

> A woman I'll call "Sarah" called me one month after the birth of her son, whom she hadn't been able to name because a numerologist told her the name she'd chosen (and loved because it felt right) was a "bad" name and would give her son a difficult life. Of course this terrified Sarah, and wanting to be a good mother, she chose not to

use that name. The problem was, she couldn't find another that felt right for her son.

The name she'd originally chosen and was told was "bad" was a Master Number 11/2 Destiny, and even though this can indicate challenges along the path to self-mastery, this soul knew what he was doing and had a prechosen agenda to fulfill in this life. This was an evolved soul who'd chosen to come back and live his life to uplift, empower, and inspire others; however, outside interference altered the course of his life.

Because of an outsider's interpretation, the world is one peace-making, inspirational leader and healer short, and this soul is walking a different path. It wasn't my place to tell Sarah what she should or shouldn't do; besides, she was too frightened to use her original name after everything she'd been told. A few weeks later, she chose another name for her baby, and his life took a different turn. Only the baby's soul can determine whether this was for the better or worse.

There's no stronger bond than the psychic-cord connection between a mother and her unborn child. So, if you're a mother-to-be, talk to your baby regularly throughout the pregnancy, and ask him or her to communicate his or her preferred name loud and clear to you. Then ask your baby's (and your own) spirit guides, angels, and helpers to ensure that you get it right.

Parenting Tips

It's important for us as caregivers and parents to recognize our children as the individual souls they are. Just like us, they have their own soul contracts to fulfill and life lessons to master. Too often we torment ourselves with guilt because we're unable to protect them from a particular challenge or painful life experience. Yet in reality, what we're doing is failing to recognize that, just like us, they came here to learn from *every* life experience—not just the happy ones. They came to experience the good, the bad, and the ugly for the evolution of their souls.

At times we may go overboard trying to protect them, yet on another level, what we're really doing is underestimating their strength and ability to make it through their challenging life experiences. When your children are faced with difficult situations, you must be there by their sides to assist as best you can, but you must also try to see their situations from another point of view. You must have faith in their ability to overcome whatever comes their way and focus your attention on a *positive* outcome and solution, rather than what you *fear* might happen.

Because you attract what you focus your attention on the most, when you focus the *majority of your attention* on your children's ability to overcome their challenges, rather than the pain they may experience along the way, you'll help them make it through unscathed. By focusing on their strength and ability to find harmonious solutions, you'll increase their inclination to attract favorable outcomes. Every parent fears for his or her children; however, your worries and trepidation only make matters worse. It's up to you as a parent to hold the light and be strong on behalf of your kids. Along with your love, time, attention, guidance, and support, having faith in your children's ability to overcome their life lessons and fulfill their life purpose is the greatest gift a parent can give.

So with that being said, let's take a look at the Child Number meanings and parenting tips for each number. These descriptions apply predominantly to the Life Path and Destiny Numbers, which are the most prominent energies in the chart. Although they can also be applied to the other Core Numbers in the chart, they will have a milder influence over the child. In order to get a complete and accurate reading of a child (or adult), his or her entire numerology and astrology profile must be taken into consideration. Feel free to read the adult number descriptions in Part I for further insight, and apply them to a child.

Parenting Tips for Each Number

1 Child

These children's destiny and life purpose is to walk the path of the Independent Individual, and they're here to embrace their individuality so they can break away from the pack. These kids will assert their authority and autonomy from an early age, and depending on their astrological profile and the other numbers in their chart, they'll want to be the boss. Although these children are determined and strong-minded, they may also battle with insecurity and self-doubt; therefore, they'll need constant encouragement and reassurance to help them believe in themselves. The best way to parent these kids is to urge them to be independent and make their own decisions. You'll need to teach them how to cooperate and appreciate the needs of others, as one of their life lessons is to learn to harmonize with others rather than boss them around. These kids need to be encouraged to walk the path less traveled and to have enough faith in themselves to embrace their uniqueness.

2 Child

These children's destiny and life purpose is to walk the path of the Cooperative Peacemaker, and they're here to promote harmony and cooperation within their family and environment. These kids are extremely loving and kind and have a great need for affection and friendship. They're extremely sensitive, creative, and intuitive, and must reside within a harmonious environment. When *not* in such an environment, they'll absorb the negative energy like a sponge. They may have food sensitivities or suffer from nervousness or allergies. They may also use food as a form of comfort or as an emotional crutch. The best way to parent these children is through love, support, friendship, and emotional connection. They're going to need help with their self-confidence and shyness, so try not to force them into things or push them too hard. These

221

children don't like to be in trouble and won't take very long to apologize if they've done something wrong. The worst thing you can do is make them suffer at length without your forgiveness. Music and various forms of creative expression are extremely beneficial to these kids.

3 Child

These children's life purpose is to walk the path of the Self-Expressive Creative, and they're here to uplift others with their artistic ability and/or use of the spoken or written word. These children can light up a room. They're bright and bubbly big talkers with short attention spans, but they're extremely playful and fun. They may be hypersensitive to criticism and may experience emotional highs and lows. These kids are the artists, actors, dancers, musicians, comedians, and entertainers of the world and should be encouraged to pursue the literary, visual, or performing arts. The best way to parent these children is with love and discipline and clearly defined boundaries. One of their life lessons is to learn to focus and prioritize, so they must be encouraged to be responsible and to follow through with their goals and plans. You'll also need to encourage them to identify their feelings and put them into words. Counseling, journaling, singing, songwriting, blogging, rapping, and poetry can be extremely therapeutic for these kids. Even though they're nonstop talkers, avoid telling them to "be quiet" unless it's absolutely necessary.

4 Child

These children's life purpose is to walk the path of the Dedicated Worker who will bring security, organization, and order to the world. Depending on their astrology profile and the other numbers in their chart, these kids may not be overly emotional and may be quite serious at times; however, they're extremely trustworthy, honest, and conscientious about doing the right thing. These children are hardworking, meticulous, and obedient and should do well in school. The best way to parent these kids is through stability, order, and routine. These children thrive in stable environments, and they need to feel safe and secure; therefore, it's important to stick to a schedule and keep things harmonious in the home. One of their life lessons is to learn to persevere through difficulties, so it pays to teach them to be optimistic and to see the positive side of life. With effort, discipline, and determination, these children can pave the way to successful careers for themselves.

5 Child

These children's life purpose is to walk the path of the Freedom-Loving Adventurer so they can gain as much life experience as they possibly can. Like number 3s, these kids are also big talkers with short attention spans, but they're extremely intelligent and clever and have a variety of talents. These kids need constant stimulation; otherwise, they can misbehave out of boredom. The best way to parent these children is to establish clearly defined boundaries, yet give them enough freedom to safely explore and experience life. These kids love to learn new things and are always asking *Why?* So encourage them to study and learn as much as they can about a subject before they get bored and throw in the towel. Number 5s will want to explore anything that stimulates their senses, so keep a close eye on them as they approach their experimental teens. Even though they're nonstop talkers, avoid telling them to "be quiet."

6 Child

These children's life purpose is to walk the path of the Responsible Caregiver so they can serve, nurture, and support others with love. Relationships are extremely important to these kids, and they need to feel like they're valued members of their family and circle of friends. These children are affectionate, creative, and musical. They make wonderful caregivers and helpers, and loyal, loving friends. The best way to parent these children is through gentleness and friendship, with plenty of one-on-one time to bond and cement your relationship. These kids are perfectionists, with very high standards for both others and themselves; therefore, teaching them to accept their imperfections and those of others will help them eliminate unnecessary disappointment and stress. They often feel they can never be, do, give, or achieve enough and may have a tendency to give up if their results are not 100 percent perfect. So show them that their best efforts are good enough in *your* eyes and that they will always be heroes for trying. These children love being in charge of others and thrive when given extra responsibilities. So assign them extra-special duties and watch them shine!

7 Child

These children's life purpose is to walk the path of the Contemplative Truth Seeker so they can hone their craft and discover their spiritual truth. Quiet time alone is extremely important for these kids. They love to gather data, read, or study anything that stimulates their minds. Depending on their astrology profile and the other numbers in their chart, they may appear quiet or emotionally detached at times, and they may take a while to warm up to others, but they're highly intuitive and intelligent. Some of the areas in which they can excel include science, technology, research, analytics, psychology, health, and metaphysics. The best way to parent these children is to allow them to be themselves. There's no need to force them into social situations if they don't feel inclined to enter them. Don't worry if they don't "fit in," as they are perfectly fine on their own. They'll eventually establish their niche and discover where they belong. Since their life purpose is to discover their spiritual truth, it's important to teach them about the universal laws and the secrets and mysteries of the

Universe. These children make wonderful students and academics, so encourage their education so they can eventually become specialists in their chosen fields.

8 Child

These children's life purpose is to walk the path of the Business-Minded Leader so they can lead, manage, or simply assist others who are less capable than they are. These kids have the potential to succeed in self-employment or the business world in general, so they're usually natural-born leaders from a very early age. Even though they can be strong-minded and abrupt, they're extremely loyal, thoughtful, and kind. Since 8 is a karmic number that's ruled by the Law of Cause and Effect, the best way to parent these children is teach them to live with honesty and integrity at all times. As 8 is also the number of manifestation, it pays to emphasize to them that their *thoughts become things*—so they can manifest their desires, rather than their fears. Because they were born with a powerful ability to attract wealth and abundance, by teaching them how to manage their money and adopt a positive mind-set, you'll increase their potential for success. These children thrive when given the opportunity to earn pocket money from doing odd jobs around the house or from an after-school job.

9 Child

These children's life purpose is to walk the path of the Compassionate Humanitarian so they can develop a high degree of empathy, understanding, and tolerance toward others, which isn't an easy task. These kids are very creative and may be drawn to the literary, performing, or visual arts. Even though they're extremely generous and loving, they can also have one heck of a temper. These kids are very sympathetic and will stick up for the underdog and the kid being bullied at school. The best way to parent them is to expose them to the diverse ways of life in this multicultural world. Encourage them to express themselves creatively or musically, and support their artistic pursuits. Due to their extreme sensitivity, you need to be mindful of the way you speak to these children. They respond best to encouragement, praise, and recognition. By teaching them how to be loving, understanding, and compassionate toward others, you'll help them fulfill their life purpose and inspire them to want to make a difference in the world.

MASTER NUMBER CHILDREN

Master Number 11/2, 22/4, and 33/6 children are evolved souls who vibrate at a high frequency and intensity. This affords them much opportunity for success in their later years, provided that they can "master" the intensity of their Master Number energy. Until that time, they'll revert to the lower vibration of their base numbers: 2, 4, and 6.

It's a great honor to parent Master Number children, and by reading this book, you're already helping them fulfill their destiny and life purpose simply by recognizing what that destiny and life purpose is. Now that you've read about Master Numbers in Part I and understand what they represent, you can help your kids reach their full potential and live by their higher ideals.

These children are hypersensitive and run on nervous energy; therefore, it's your responsibility to teach them how to harness, channel, and express that energy in a healthy way. Repressed nervous energy, or energy of this kind that is expressed in negative ways, can result in panic attacks, anxiety, phobias, skin conditions, allergies, addictions, and unusual medical conditions. Therefore, a positive mind-set, coupled with an understanding of the energetic system within the human body (and Universe), is essential for children with Master Numbers. Typically, those with strong, confident, and grounded astrology charts and Core Numbers don't experience the same levels of sensitivity and anxiety.

Regular exercise (preferably cardiovascular); dance; music; creativity; and the literary, visual, and performing arts can help these kids express their energy in positive ways. A clean, healthy diet; spending time in nature and the outdoors; the companionship of a beloved pet; close friendships; a loving family; and a harmonious home life will help keep them balanced, centered, and grounded. Teaching your Master Number children relaxation and breathing techniques, EFT (Emotional Freedom Technique), visualization, prayer, and meditation will calm their nerves and improve their self-esteem. It will also help them channel their intense creative energy toward their hopes and dreams.

These children benefit greatly from self-esteem classes and adopting a spiritual faith from an early age. So teach them about their spirit guides and angels, especially Archangels Michael and Metatron, whom they can call on anytime for guidance and protection. I know that with my own children, this has helped immensely. It also pays to teach these kids about the universal laws, especially the principles behind the Law of Attraction. As a result, they can live in alignment with the Divine and manifest their desires rather than their fears.

Master Number children are blessed and have much potential for success. So honor and cherish every moment you're together, and try to be as patient and understanding as you can. It may not be easy for either you or your child at times, and you'll be tested along the way. However, you have a prechosen soul contract together, and there will be many rewarding experiences to come.

Master 11/2 Child

As 11 is a higher octave of number 2, read the 2 Child description for greater understanding and insight.

These children's life purpose is to walk the path of the Inspirational Teacher, with the potential to become a spiritual messenger, should they choose that option. These kids are extremely intuitive, perceptive, and wise and have an understanding beyond their years that enables them to see the bigger picture of what's going on around them. These children are emotional, empathetic, and kind. However, depending on their astrology profile and the other numbers in their charts, they may suffer from shyness or a lack of self-esteem. They have leadership qualities brewing beneath the surface, but need the courage and self-confidence to bring them through.

The best way to parent these children is by being open-minded and understanding. If they're self-conscious and insecure, teach them to focus on their strengths rather than their shortcomings. These kids have the ability to manifest their thoughts into reality, so they must be taught from an early age that *thoughts become things.* Because they're strongly governed by the Law of Cause and Effect, they must be encouraged to live with honesty and integrity at all times. Be mindful that these kids may stretch the truth or try to manipulate situations to their advantage, so it's important to create an environment where they feel safe to speak their truth.

Master 22/4 Child

As 22 is a higher octave of number 4, read the 4 Child description for greater understanding and insight.

These children's life purpose is to walk the path of the Master Builder, who has the potential to create or govern something for the benefit of humankind. Depending on the astrology profile and the other numbers in their charts, these kids are either hardworking visionaries or appear indifferent and detached. Some 22/4 children are hypersensitive and timid, whereas others seem emotionally controlled and contained; however, regardless of their emotional disposition, all are incredibly perceptive and deep. With love, support, and understanding, these children have the ability to accomplish anything they set their minds to.

These kids have the ability to bring dreams to fruition with their logical, practical, and methodical approach—provided that they don't allow their insecurities and perfectionism to get the better of them. The best way to parent these children is with love, support, patience, and understanding. If they seem emotionally awkward or detached, don't assume that they love you any less. These kids thrive when they're encouraged to express themselves creatively. They have an abundance of love to give and would benefit greatly from the company and friendship of a pet. A good education is vital for these kids. When you teach them to balance their sensitivity and intuition with logic and reason, they can reach their full potential.

Master 33/6 Child

As 33 is a higher octave of number 6, read the 6 Child description for greater understanding and insight.

These children's life purpose is to walk the path of the Cosmic Parent, with the potential to become a Master of Healing Energies, should they so choose. They're talented caregivers and entertainers, with an inclination to help others and a desire to cheer them up. These kids are very creative and may be artistically or musically gifted in some way. They're outgoing, helpful, and friendly, and are valued family members and friends. Babies, toddlers, and young children enjoy being in the company of 33/6 children because they're fun, playful, and charismatic and have that "certain something."

The best way to parent these kids is to teach them that they don't have to be 100 perfect all of the time, as they set very high standards for themselves that can cause them much distress. They often feel they're not being, doing, giving, or achieving enough and need to be taught how to define their personal boundaries and embrace their imperfections. Journaling, poetry, singing, songwriting, rapping, playing an instrument, dance, and acting are healthy and enjoyable ways for 33/6 children to express their thoughts and feelings. It isn't unusual for them to pursue a career in health/beauty; counseling; or the literary, visual, or performing arts. Encouraging them to love themselves and others unconditionally and to assist those in need will help them fulfill their destiny and life purpose.

+ + +

Number-Conscious Living

Now that you know all about the children in your life, let's take a look at your house and its associated numbers. After that, please read on for further information on other meaningful numbers in your life.

HOUSE NUMBERS AND STREET NAME NUMBERS

Just like businesses, pets, and people, houses have numerology blueprints, too. But when it comes to the numerology of a home, it's not so much the House Number itself that influences your life—it's how you behave under that vibration that will have the greatest effect. Despite the number on the outside of the house, the most dominant energy of all is the energy of the *people within*. In other words, the energy and intention of the inhabitants is the major determinant of the energy of the home, regardless of its number. For example, a person may move into an 8 house (the money number) hoping to generate wealth and abundance, but if that person has a negative mind-set about money, he or she will undoubtedly remain financially challenged despite living in a "money house."

It pays to bear this in mind if you're moving into a home in the hopes that the House Number alone is going to help you achieve your goals. In order to attain what you desire while living somewhere, you must meet the Universe halfway by focusing your own personal energy (your thoughts and emotions) on manifesting your dreams. You need to put in the effort, because the number of your house can't manifest on its own.

On the other hand, the number energy of a home will have a natural effect on its inhabitants, so it pays to understand the nature of that energy (number) so you can use it to your advantage. Once you've made an intuitive decision about the ideal home to move into, you can then familiarize yourself with its number to accentuate the positives and minimize the challenges.

Sometimes a House Number can support your destiny or other numbers in your chart, and other times it can bring in a number you're lacking and need to develop in this life. If your House Number is considered a challenge, it can help you overcome major lessons while living in that home.

Choosing a Home

When choosing a home, the number one rule is to go by how you *feel*—before consulting the numbers. Only your soul knows the future life experiences you've yet to encounter, and only your soul knows the ideal home to support you through those experiences. Therefore, only your soul (via your intuition) can guide you toward your perfect home. In the initial stages of choosing where to live, your intuition is more important than the House Number that your ego mind assumes will suit you best. So before you calculate the numbers of your potential home, ask yourself these questions:

- *How does this home make me feel?*
- *Does it feel like my next home?*

- *Can I see myself living here?*

- *Do I feel safe here?*

- *What do I hope to accomplish in this home?*

- *Can I see myself taking steps toward my goals while living here?*

As you spend quiet time alone contemplating or meditating on these questions, your intuition will tell you whether it's the ideal home to choose. You'll get a strong feeling—an inner knowing that it is the perfect home for you. Remember to ask the Universe (God/Source/Divine), plus your spirit guides, angels, and loved ones in spirit, for assistance in helping you decide. Then ask for a sign as confirmation that you're on the right path.

※

Now let's find out how to calculate a House Number. In numerology, the House Number reveals the energy of the house, and the Street Name Number reveals the energy of the street. The House Number has the greatest influence of all, because it relates directly to the space you occupy and reveals what you can expect while living there.

How to Calculate a House Number

To calculate a House Number, simply add all of the mailbox numbers together and then reduce to a single-digit House Number. For example, 4506 Main Street would be:

4+5+0+6 = 15
1+5 = **6 House Number**

When calculating a house number where additional letters or numbers are included in the address—such as 6/564 Main Street or 32B Main Street—there are two calculation theories among

233

numerologists. The first is to include those letters or numbers in your calculation, creating one overall number, as shown below:

For example, 6/564 Main Street would be:

6+5+6+4 = 21
2+1 = **3 House Number**

and 32B Main Street would be:

3+2+2 (because *B* = 2) = **7 House Number**

The second theory is to calculate the house or apartment number and the additional letters or numbers separately.

For example, 32B Main Street would be:

3+2 = **5 House Number** (which applies to every house/apartment included in the shared address "32 Main Street")

and B = a **2 overtone** (which applies specifically to Apartment B)

Therefore 32B Main Street is a *5 House Number* with an additional *2 overtone* that applies specifically to house B and differentiates it from all other houses within the 32 Main Street complex.

If your House Number totals 11, 22, or 33, it becomes an 11/2, 22/4, or 33/6 House Number. When the House Number (prior to breaking down) is composed of multiple numbers, such as number 385, it pays to take each individual number into consideration and investigate separately for additional information, as each one of those numbers (that is, 3, 8, and 5) will have an effect on the home.

✳

Now, let's take a look at the House Number meanings and the positive and challenging aspects of each one.

House Number Meanings

1 House Number

A 1 House Number promotes strength, independence, and individuality. It's the ideal home for those who wish to stand on their own two feet, be self-motivated, and accomplish their goals. If you like to live alone or prefer to work from home (especially as an independent contractor), a 1 House Number is the perfect one for you. This house will inspire many creative and innovative ideas, but be mindful of competitiveness, aggressiveness, and self-centeredness, or becoming overambitious.

2 House Number

A 2 House Number promotes partnership, sensitivity, and healing. It's the ideal home for couples and those who like nurturing and helping others. If you have a love of animals and enjoy creating a beautiful garden, a 2 House Number is the perfect one for you. A 2 home lends itself to home-cooked meals, music, psychic development, and home-based healing businesses. This house promotes cooperation, compromise, and understanding of others, but be mindful of heightened emotions, jealousy, codependency, and giving too much of yourself to others.

3 House Number

A 3 House Number promotes creativity, communication, and laughter. It's the ideal home for artistic people looking to enhance their creative abilities. If you like to write, cook, decorate, design, paint, sing, dance, or create something using your imagination or your hands, a 3 House Number is the perfect one for you. This house promotes fun, happiness, and joy; therefore, it's a wonderful vibration for raising children and entertaining family and friends. On the downside, it can also encourage criticism, gossip, emotional highs and lows, and irresponsible behavior.

4 House Number

A 4 House Number promotes structure, order, and stability. It's the ideal home for those who want to build a solid foundation for their future and who require the mental and physical discipline to do so. If you're looking to settle down and create more security in your life, a 4 House Number is the perfect one for you. This is a good old-fashioned family home that will enable you to commit yourself to your goals. Be mindful that 4 also indicates that extra mental, physical, and emotional effort is required to get results, so it's essential that you work hard and make time for fun and relaxation while living in this home.

5 House Number

A 5 House Number promotes change, activity, and adventure. It's the ideal home for those who like to travel and get the most out of life. There will be a lot going on and plenty of ups and downs; however, there will be no shortage of excitement to keep you on your toes. If you're looking to get as many experiences as you possibly can out of this life, a 5 House Number is the perfect one for you. Communication flows in this house, but be mindful of overindulgence and erratic or extravagant behavior. Extra effort will be required to focus and achieve your goals.

6 House Number

A 6 House Number promotes love, beauty, and friendship. It is the ideal home in which to raise a family and establish close relationships with others. Children, animals, and gardens thrive in the energy of a 6 home, as it feels comforting and inviting to all. If you're looking for a house to teach you about love and beauty and to inspire your creativity, a 6 House Number is the perfect one for you. This is the ideal house for a home-based beauty, child-care, cooking, clothing, counseling, or healing business, but be mindful of perfectionism. Try to avoid becoming a martyr and over-interfering in others' problems while living in this home.

7 House Number

A 7 House Number promotes introspection, contemplation, and personal growth. It's the ideal home for those who like to relax and spend quiet time alone. If you're looking for a suitable environment in which to study and become a specialist in your craft, a 7 House Number is the perfect one for you. Spiritual growth is inevitable, as 7 will encourage you to discover your spiritual truth while living under its vibration. This is the ideal home for metaphysicians, healers, analysts, philosophers, reporters, doctors, scientists, technicians, teachers, students, and loners, but it can be a challenging vibration for couples and families. These challenges can be overcome when extra effort is made to communicate and stay connected to loved ones who reside within the home.

8 House Number

An 8 House Number promotes abundance, recognition, and power. It's the ideal home for high achievers, entrepreneurs, and those who are dedicated to their careers. If you're looking to rise to a position of authority or to manifest wealth and abundance, an 8 House Number is the perfect one for you. Provided that you have a positive mind-set, live with honesty and integrity, balance the material and spiritual worlds, and develop a healthy relationship with money, this house can help you manifest your dreams. Be mindful of a reversal of fortune while living in this home, and keep your finances in order. Don't let money, image, status, or power define you.

9 House Number

A 9 House Number promotes wisdom, compassion, tolerance, and transformation. It's the ideal home for those who wish to serve humanity, the community, or simply those in need. If you have a love of animals or the arts and are a humanitarian at heart, a 9 House Number is the perfect one for you. This home focuses on healing and closure and will encourage you to forgive and heal your past. You'll reach a high level of awareness and understanding while living in this home, but be mindful of intense and extreme emotions, including impatience and frustration.

MASTER NUMBER HOUSE NUMBERS

Just as Master Numbers apply to people, they apply to houses as well. If your home has an 11/2, 22/4, or 33/6 House Number, these number meanings will give you an idea as to what you can expect while living in this home.

11/2 House Number

Read 2 House Number, also.

An 11/2 House Number promotes higher learning and spiritual wisdom. It's the ideal home for those wishing to attain self-mastery and reach elevated levels of awareness. This house focuses on self-love and understanding, as well as healing, spiritual, psychic, and personal development; however, you may encounter many lessons along the way.

22/4 House Number

Read 4 House Number, also.

A 22/4 House Number enhances the ability to build, create, or promote something that benefits the community or humanity. It's the ideal home for those who wish to attain self-mastery and accomplish their goals. This home focuses on bringing ideas into physical form; however, your faith, dedication, and commitment may be tested along the way.

33/6 House Number

Read 6 House Number, also.

A 33/6 House Number promotes the ability to heal and up-lift everyone who passes through the door. It's the ideal home for those with a love of children, music, beauty, food, entertaining, teaching, laughter, creativity, and the arts. This home will amplify your emotions, so be prepared to deal with your unresolved issues once and for all.

KARMIC DEBT HOUSE NUMBERS

Just as Karmic Debt Numbers apply to people, they apply to houses as well. If you're living in a 13, 14, 16 or 19 House Number, you'll want to be mindful of ways to help raise the vibration of your home.

13/4 House Number

Read 4 House Number, also.

While living in this home, it pays to live with honesty and integrity at all times and to face your challenges head-on rather than succumb to quick-fix solutions or shortcuts. With self-discipline, tenacity, and drive, you will greatly improve your experience in this house. A 13/4 House Number brings an opportunity for personal transformation where effort and determination are the keys to your success. By using your words to uplift and inspire others rather than to gossip, criticize, or complain, you'll raise the vibration of this home.

14/5 House Number

Read 5 House Number, also.

While living in this home, it pays to exercise temperance and moderation in every area of your life and be mindful of over-indulgence. By taking your responsibilities seriously and honoring your commitments, you'll greatly improve your experience in this house. A 14/5 House Number brings an opportunity for personal transformation where self-discipline and accountability are the keys to your success. By balancing your desire for freedom and adventure with your responsibilities, you'll raise the vibration of this home.

16/7 House Number

Read 7 House Number, also.

While living in this home, try to reevaluate your core values and eliminate any superficial foundations that don't align with your higher self. By recognizing and rising above any ego-driven thoughts and behaviors, you'll greatly improve your experience in this house. A 16/7 House Number brings an opportunity for personal transformation where humility, honesty, loyalty, and au-thenticity are the keys to your success. By focusing on your personal development and surrendering to the unexpected events in your life, you'll raise the vibration of this home.

19/1 House Number

Read 1 House Number, also.

While living in this home, try to admit your mistakes and see other people's points of view regardless of whether they're right or wrong. By considering others' opinions and accepting assistance when it's offered, you'll greatly improve your experience in this house. A 19/1 House Number brings an opportunity for personal transformation where compassion and compromise are the keys to your success. By taking other people's wants and needs into consideration as well as your own, you'll raise the vibration of this home.

※

Now that you're familiar with the energy of your home, let's take a look at the energy of your street.

How to Calculate a Street Name Number

A Street Name Number is calculated using the same formula to calculate a person's Destiny Number.

The influence of a Street Name Number is minor in comparison to the House Number; however, it pays to know what it is to get a feel for the energy of the street. If you live in a named apartment or housing complex (such as Garden Village Apartments), you will need to calculate the apartment or complex name as well.

When calculating a Street Name Number, be sure to use the name that appears on the street sign.

Please note: *Master Numbers and Karmic Debt Numbers do not apply to Street Name Numbers.*

Let's use "Main St" and the adding-across method as an example.

M A I N S T
4+1+9+5 1+2 = 22

2+2 = 4 Street Name Number

Did you notice I used *Main St* rather than *Main Street* in the example? This is because *Main St* is the name that appears on the street sign. Street names that include numbers in the title such as "63rd St" are calculated like so: $6 + 3 + 9$ *(R)* = 4 *(D)* = 22 . . . 2 + 2 = **4 Street Name Number.**

✻

Here's a rough guideline of the Street Name Number meanings.

Street Name Number Meanings

1 Street Name Number

This street may stand out or be unique in some way. It encourages individuality and independence, and is ideal for a home-based business and self-starters.

2 Street Name Number

This street may feel homey and comforting in some way. It encourages sensitivity and cooperation, and is ideal for a home-based business, couples, and families.

3 Street Name Number

This street may be popular and full of activity. It encourages self-expression and communication, and is ideal for creative residents who enjoy hosting social gatherings.

4 Street Name Number

This street may feel grounded and down-to-earth. It encourages commitment and discipline, and is ideal for those who wish to stabilize and settle down.

5 Street Name Number

This street may be full of activity and have a lot going on. It encourages progress, movement, and change, and is ideal for active people on the move.

6 Street Name Number

This street may feel homey and welcoming in some way. It encourages friendship and domestic responsibility, and is ideal for a home-based business, couples, roommates, and families.

7 Street Name Number

This street may feel private and mysterious. It encourages contemplation and study, and is ideal for academics and professionals.

8 Street Name Number

This street may exude status, strength, or power in some way. It encourages responsibility and manifestation, and is ideal for a home-based business and entrepreneurs.

9 Street Name Number

This street may be multicultural or community focused in some way. It encourages tolerance and broadmindedness, and is ideal for families, artists, and humanitarians.

✳

Once you know your House Number and Street Name Number, you can add the two together for an overall evaluation of your address.

Let's take a look at calculating your Address Number now.

How to Calculate an Address Number

There are two ways to calculate your Address Number to obtain an evaluation of your overall address.

Please note: *Master Numbers and Karmic Debt Numbers do not apply to Address Numbers.*

Method 1

Simply add your House Number and Street Name Number (and the number of the name of your complex, where applicable) together to create one overall Address Number.

Let's use 32B Main St as an example:

32 (5) + B (2) + Main St (4) = 11

1+1 = 2 Address Number

Method 2

Another option is to evaluate your address by individual segments rather than an overall total.

Let's use 32B Main St as an example once again:

32B Main St is a *5 house* on a *4 street* with a *2 overtone* that differentiates it from the other apartments at 32 Main St.

How you choose to calculate an address is entirely up to you. As with everything else in numerology, there isn't a right or wrong answer. Refer to the House Number descriptions for the Address Number meanings and apply them to your overall address.

✳

Try not get too caught up in the numbers of your street and home, as your personal numerology profile has a far greater influence on your life. Don't worry if you don't like your House or Street Name Number, because there's no such thing as a "bad" number. Each one has benefits, strengths, and challenges. Despite the number or appearance of your home, always be thankful for the comfort and shelter it provides you. Sadly, there are millions of people in the world who don't have the luxury of a home.

If you'd like to remove negative energy from your home or to raise its energy vibration, why not consider a house clearing? The energy from people, experiences, illnesses, arguments, and emotions (such as anger, fear, heartache, and depression) can linger within your home, as it does in every space. A house clearing is the process of clearing away any toxic or stagnant energy while evoking new, positive, and uplifting energy to replace it.

You can Google "house clearing" to learn how to do this yourself or to find a specialist in your area. House clearing can also be done remotely if there's nobody to assist you in your neck of the woods, but be sure to choose somebody with legitimate credentials and testimonials. Feng shui is another wonderful tool that can help you enhance the positive energy flow within your home. For further information about feng shui, I recommend you read *Feng Shui Simply,* by Cheryl Grace.

✳

Now, for those who are thinking of getting married, let's take a look at Wedding Day Numbers.

WEDDING DAY NUMBERS

A wedding day is considered one of the most important dates in one's life, when nothing else matters except the celebration of love and commitment between two people. But as glamorous as it sounds, a wedding is also one of the most stressful life events, where it's absolutely essential that everything go according to plan. Now, I have to stress that a Wedding Day Number isn't going to make or break a marriage; however, it can add an extra element of magic to your special day and play an important role in how the day itself unfolds. If you're in a position to choose your wedding day, why not consult the numbers to give it the best possible chance for success?

How to Calculate a Wedding Day Number

A Wedding Day Number is calculated by adding the numbers in the wedding date.

Step 1

Add all the numbers of your wedding date together using your preferred calculation method, whether it be reducing down or adding across.

246

Step 2

Reduce any double-digit numbers down to get a single-digit Wedding Day Number. Number 11, 22, or 33 reduces down to a 2, 4, or 6 Wedding Day Number.

For example, using the adding-across method, a June 20, 2014 (6-20-2014), wedding day would be:

6+2+0+2+0+1+4 = 15
1+5 = **6 Wedding Day**

Let's take a look at the Wedding Day Number meanings.

Wedding Day Number Meanings

1 Wedding Day Number

The number 1 represents new beginnings, so this is the perfect day to embark upon a new life together. This day will definitely stand out and make its mark on the world. One thing's for certain: this wedding will be unique.

2 Wedding Day Number

The number 2 represents partnership, so this is the perfect day to celebrate the ultimate partnership: *marriage.* A 2 day also relates to the emotions, so there isn't a better way to express your feelings of love and appreciation than by marrying the one you love. This is a very favorable day to marry!

3 Wedding Day Number

The number 3 represents celebration, so this is the perfect day to celebrate a marriage with family and friends. It is also the number of joy, happiness, and laughter—all the key ingredients that make for a fabulous wedding. This will be a joyous occasion that will be remembered for years to come.

4 Wedding Day Number

The number 4 represents commitment and stability, so this is the perfect day to start building the foundation of your future together. As 4 also represents attention to detail, be sure to cross your *t*'s and dot your *i*'s when planning your big day to ensure you cover all your bases.

5 Wedding Day Number

The number 5 represents change and unexpected events, so if things need to go according to plan, you might want to consider another day. On the other hand, it could be a pleasant, unexpected event that makes your wedding day the most exciting day of your life.

6 Wedding Day Number

The number 6 represents love, so this is the ultimate day to exchange vows and recognize the love you have for one another. This is also the number of family and friendship, so it's the perfect day to celebrate a marriage with the loved ones in your life. Of all the days to choose from, I recommend 6 (and 2) over all others.

7 Wedding Day Number

The number 7 represents spirituality, so this is a good day for a religious or spiritually based ceremony to celebrate your love. To raise the vibration of the wedding day itself, consider including a group blessing, prayer, or meditation in the ceremony.

8 Wedding Day Number

The number 8 represents money and recognition, so be mindful of going over budget for the sake of keeping up appearances. This is also the number of manifestation, so visualize a perfect wedding day where everything unfolds as you wish. Be honest in all your wedding-day dealings and everything should flow.

9 Wedding Day Number

The number 9 represents endings and completion, where it's out with the old to make way for the new. Some numerologists feel that it's unwise to begin something on a 9 day; however, a 9 day could symbolize the end of a cycle of being *unmarried!*

Day Number

Another number to take into consideration when calculating your wedding date is the Day Number, taken from the day of the month. For example:

- The 1st, 10th, 19th, or 28th day of the month is a **1** day.
- The 2nd, 11th, 20th, or 29th day of the month is a **2** day.
- The 3rd, 12th, 21st, or 30th day of the month is a **3** day.
- The 4th, 13th, 22nd, or 31st day of the month is a **4** day.
- The 5th, 14th, or 23rd day of the month is a **5** day.

- The 6th, 15th, or 24th day of the month is a **6** day.

- The 7th, 16th, or 25th day of the month is a **7** day.

- The 8th, 17th, or 26th day of the month is an **8** day.

- The 9th, 18th, or 27th day of the month is a **9** day.

Even though the energy of a Day Number isn't as strong as the Wedding Day Number, it still has an influence on the day. Because *a number has the same meaning wherever it appears,* the Wedding Day Number descriptions apply to the Day Numbers as well—but in a milder fashion.

It also pays to take your and your partner's Personal Day Numbers into consideration for good measure. But don't go overboard trying to check every box. You can make things more complicated than they need to be by overanalyzing every detail. Remember, there are billions of couples around the world who didn't consult the numbers before their wedding day and are happily married today—just as there are others who married on a 2 or 6 Wedding Day and are now divorced.

Don't be discouraged if you're unable to get married on your preferred Wedding Day Number, because the power of your intention can override the numbers. As of today, visualize your wedding day being exactly as you wish it to be and imagine everything running smoothly. As you focus on how you want your wedding day to unfold and consistently picture it in your mind, the Universe will adjust itself accordingly to make your dream come true. Regardless of what the psychics, stars, and numbers say, what you believe to be *will* be, and your intention is the key!

✵

Speaking of dreams, beliefs, and intentions, let's see how your numbers can help you manifest your dreams.

Manifestation with Numbers

Whether you're aware of it or not, *your thoughts become things.* In fact, your thoughts are magnetic signals that attract whatever you focus your attention on the most. This means that you can deliberately attract favorable opportunities to improve your quality of life simply by using the power of your mind. Provided that your desires serve your greater good and are part of your Divine plan, you have the ability to attract them into your life—in Divine order and timing.

The deliberate manifestation of your desires will involve consistent visualization, affirmations, meditation, and prayer—but not *only* that. It will involve other key ingredients that are vital to your success. Before I touch upon the manifestation tips and strengths for each number, here are some important suggestions for helping you manifest your dreams:

1. Get clear about what you want.

2. Focus the *majority* of your attention on your *desire,* rather than the *absence* of your desire or your doubts, worries, and fears. That is, concentrate on what you *do* want, rather than what you *don't* want. This is where prayer, affirmations, creative visualization, vision boards, gratitude diaries, and the like come in handy. These are manifestation tools that enable you to *give attention* to your desires.

3. Recognize and reprogram any conscious or subconscious limiting beliefs that are preventing you from attracting what you want. Modalities such as hypnosis, PSYCH-K, kinesiology, neuro-linguistic programming (NLP), Emotional Freedom Technique (EFT/tapping), and cognitive-behavioral therapy can help you achieve this.

4. Let go and surrender the outcome to Divine order and timing—and get on with your life, knowing that whatever unfolds is for your greater good.

5. Make peace with your life as it is *today* without your object of desire.

6. Live in the present moment, and find things to be grateful for, however big or small.

7. Become that which you're trying to attract. For example, if you want to attract love, you yourself need to be loving—and that means acting lovingly toward *everyone,* not just your family and friends.

8. Keep yourself inspired. Fill every possible moment with people, books, websites, seminars, memories, movies, and *anything at all* that stirs or excites you and supports your dream. I know from my own experience that listening to HayHouseRadio .com has helped keep me motivated and inspired over the years. Listening to like-minded souls discussing the Law of Attraction and other mind-body-spirit matters over the airwaves while I was home alone and in need of a spiritual pick-me-up has helped raise my vibration and keep me in the "manifestation" zone.

9. Harmonize with the universal flow of life by doing more of the things that make you *feel good*—whether it's eating ice cream, listening to music you love, watching a funny movie, or spending quality time with friends. It doesn't matter what you do, as long as it *feels good*. Manifestation is all about emotion, and when you consistently feel good, you'll attract your desired outcome sooner.

10. Accept your shortcomings, failures, losses, misfortunes, hardships, heartaches, and betrayals as quickly as you can, and express your emotions in a healthy way. Unforgiveness, self-pity, and the desire for revenge will only keep you out of alignment and prevent the manifestation of your dreams.

11. Recognize the thoughts, behaviors, circumstances, and people that create disharmony in your life. Find a way to accept them, live with them, improve them, or avoid them altogether.

12. Be as positive and healthy as you can. Have faith in yourself and be optimistic about your future. Eat healthy food; drink plenty of water; exercise regularly; listen to beautiful music; discover your spiritual truth; spend time in nature and the outdoors; pray; love and be loved; express your negative emotions in a healthy way; spend time with friends; take up meditation, yoga, conscious breathing, or qigong; learn EFT (Emotional Freedom Technique); be creative; have fun; and laugh as much as you can.

13. Love yourself unconditionally, forgive others and yourself, accept the imperfection in the world, and recognize that your ego isn't the voice of your soul.

Manifestation Tips for the Numbers

As you can see, the successful manifestation of your dreams is more than just a matter of positive thinking, doing affirmations, and visualizing—it's a mind-set! It's about raising your *overall vibration* through the way you live your life and the way you see the world.

When it comes to the manifestation of your desires, every number has strengths and challenges. In the following sections, you'll find some manifestation tips to accentuate your strengths, which in turn will increase your potential for successful manifestation. These descriptions apply predominantly to the Life Path and Destiny Numbers, but should be taken into consideration for the other Core Numbers as well. I suggest you read each of the following tips whether you have those particular numbers in your chart or not, as you will benefit from the information regardless.

Numbers 1 and 11/2

One of your greatest strengths as a 1 or 11/2 is the energy behind your thoughts. You have an incredibly powerful mind, and when your thoughts are channeled in a *positive* direction, as in visualization, you can achieve phenomenal results. As a 1 (or double 1), you excel in the creative process; however, your greatest challenge is your impatience and inability to live in the present moment while everything unfolds. You want everything to happen in *your* timing, rather than *Divine timing;* however, you need to spend less time *doing* and more time *being* in order to manifest your dreams.

You increase your ability to manifest your dreams when you channel your creative energy in a *positive* direction rather than blocking your creative flow with impatience, anxiety, insecurity, or fear. When you truly believe there's no such thing as competition in the Universe and that *what is meant for you cannot be taken away,* there's nothing you cannot be, do, or have.

*Affirmation: My positive creative
thoughts are manifesting my dreams.*

Numbers 2, 11/2, and 22/4

One of your greatest strengths as a 2, 11/2, or 22/4 is your ability to see the bigger picture and detach from the outcome while your dreams come to fruition. Your heightened sensitivity enables you to reach incredible depths of emotion during visualization, which is extremely beneficial to the creative process. Your greatest challenge, however, is your lack of self-confidence and lack of conviction that something good could actually happen to *you.* With increased confidence, unwavering faith, and belief in yourself, you can make your dreams come true.

You increase your ability to manifest your dreams when you know without a doubt that you're worthy of and deserve to live, a happy, harmonious life. When you can put your needs, hopes, and dreams above everything else without feeling guilty, you'll make those dreams come true. You have a natural affinity with the moon, so use it to give your thoughts and creations an extra boost. (See "Moon Cycles" in the "Manifestation Tools" segment to follow.)

Affirmation: I am confident, deserving,
and worthy of manifesting my dreams.

Numbers 3 and 33/6

Your greatest strength as a 3 or 33/6 is your creative imagination, emphasized by your heightened sensitivity. This enables you to visualize your desire with ease and tap into the emotion of what it would *feel like* to have it in your life. This is a very powerful combination for successful manifestation. You're a natural dreamer and actor; therefore, it's easy to "fake it 'til you make it"—that is, until you actualize your dreams. This is a valuable key ingredient in the manifestation process. Your greatest challenge is your lack of focus and inability to follow through with consistent practical action. You may change your mind about what you want or give up altogether because you become bored after a short period of time.

You increase your ability to manifest your dreams when you align yourself with the Divine through creative pursuits on a regular basis. Any form of joyful self-expression will put you in the zone of manifestation by raising your vibration. You're a born optimist who can see the light at the end of the tunnel, so be sure you look at the glass as half-full rather than focus on the drama. Remember, you're a big talker, and everything you say is an affirmation, so speak only about what you *want,* rather than what you *don't want.*

Affirmation: Through joyful creative
expression, I manifest my dreams.

Numbers 4 and 22/4

One of your greatest strengths as a 4 or 22/4 is your ability to focus and commit yourself entirely to the actualization of your dreams. It's easy for you to follow through with the necessary

255

practical action to make your dreams come true; however, your greatest challenge is your inability to believe that miracles exist in this logical, rational world. You may struggle to continue believing in your dreams when they haven't yet come to fruition. For some 4s, tapping into your emotions during visualization may be a bit of a struggle, too.

You increase your ability to manifest your dreams when you let go of your need to control each and every step of the manifestation process. When you step outside of logic and reason and surrender to the inexplicable laws of manifestation, you'll actualize your dreams and improve your quality of life. Even when there's no physical evidence or guarantee that your dream will come to fruition, you must do whatever it takes to find the courage to believe. And don't worry too much about the emotional aspect of visualization—your intention and belief are just as important as what you *feel* in your heart.

> **Affirmation:** *I have faith and trust*
> *in my ability to manifest my dreams.*

Number 5

One of your greatest strengths as a 5 is your overactive mind, because it enables you to pay constant attention to your dreams. Because you attract what you think about the most, if your mind is going to race nonstop, you might as well think about your dreams! Your greatest challenge, however, is your changeability and inability to focus; therefore, your scattered thoughts and actions tend to produce scattered results. If you commit yourself to your dream rather than quit because you're bored, with perseverance and dedication you will make that dream come true.

You increase your ability to manifest your dreams when you have enough freedom, excitement, and variety in your everyday life to keep you feeling inspired. By choosing to see the inspiration and adventure in the mundane, you'll align yourself with Source and manifest your dreams. Boredom and frustration only take you out of alignment, yet inspiration and appreciation help you attract your desires sooner. The key to making the manifestation process stimulating enough to hold your interest is to use a variety of techniques. This, combined with plain old mental discipline, will help you succeed. Consistency and focus are the keys.

*Affirmation: As I see the adventure
in everyday things, I manifest my dreams.*

Numbers 6 and 33/6

One of your greatest strengths as a 6 or 33/6 is your commitment to manifesting your dreams. Your steadfast dedication enables you to set a powerful intention and hold that vision in your mind until it comes to fruition. While you flawlessly cross your *t*'s, dot your *i*'s, and do everything you can do to actualize your dreams, your challenge is your idealism and perfectionism and the need for everything to be just right. When things don't turn out exactly as you planned, you find it hard to accept, let go, and move on. Yet acceptance and yielding are vital ingredients for successful manifestation.

You increase your ability to manifest your dreams when you surrender the outcome and know that in Divine order and timing, everything will fall into place. When you trust that the Universe knows more than you do and allow it to take care of the details (rather than trying to control everything yourself), you'll attract your desired outcome sooner. As soon as you accept the imperfection in yourself, others, and the world, you'll increase the synchronicity in your life and make your dreams come true.

*Affirmation: I accept that imperfection
is perfect as I manifest my dreams.*

Number 7

One of your greatest strengths as a 7 is your intuition and your natural ability to understand the universal laws. Because your life purpose is to discover your spiritual truth, you were born knowing that you're a spiritual being having a human experience, rather than a human being having a spiritual experience. You intuitively believe in a greater power and the existence of miracles in everyday life—but, paradoxically, your greatest challenge of all is your lack of faith in the Universe, combined with your lack of belief in *yourself*. Even though you want to believe in the Universe's potential and your ability to manifest your dreams, your underlying pessimistic nature may convince you that it's too good to be true.

You increase your ability to manifest your dreams when you remove yourself from the hustle and bustle of everyday life to spend quiet alone time in meditation and prayer. As you strengthen your relationship with the Divine, you strengthen your relationship with *yourself*. By spending more time in nature and the outdoors, you'll develop the necessary level of self-trust that enables you to make your dreams come true. As you purify your vibration and explore metaphysical pursuits, you'll align yourself with Source and actualize your dreams.

Affirmation: I have faith and trust in the
Universe and myself, and I manifest my dreams.

Number 8

The number 8 is all about manifestation; therefore, one of your greatest strengths is the power behind your thoughts. Because you can manifest with ease, your greatest gift and strength is your greatest burden as well. On the one hand, you can make your dreams come true with ease, but on the other, you can easily manifest your fears. Because 8 is also the number of karmic balance that governs the Law of Cause and Effect, you must be conscious of the motivations behind everything you do.

You increase your ability to manifest your dreams when you minimize your fears and pay attention to your thoughts at all times. By training yourself to focus the majority of your attention on what you *want,* rather than what you *fear,* you'll attract less of what you *don't want* and more of what you *do.* In other words, if you don't want something in your life, don't give it your attention. As an 8, you'll find that a positive mind-set, combined with a healthy relationship with money, is essential to your success. When you adopt an attitude of abundance and *believe* that the Universe is abundant, you'll attract abundance into your life. Because you're strongly governed by the Law of Cause and Effect, you must strive to live with honesty and integrity at all times.

*Affirmation: As I focus on what
I want, I manifest my dreams.*

Number 9

One of your greatest strengths as a 9 is your intense passion, as it's that very same passion—combined with your vivid imagination, intense emotions, and relentless determination and drive—that will make your dreams come true. Your greatest challenge, however, is your inability to move past your frustration when things don't go according to plan. The intensity of your anger or disappointment alone will prevent the manifestation of your dreams.

You increase your ability to manifest your dreams when you can accept, let go, and move on when things don't turn out as anticipated. *Acceptance* and *surrender* are two necessary ingredients in the manifestation process—*acceptance* that whatever happens is for your greater good even if it you can't see it at the time, and having the ability to *surrender* the outcome to the Divine while knowing in your heart that what is meant for you cannot be taken away. Desperation delays manifestation, so if you want to manifest your dreams, you need to make peace with where you are *today.*

Affirmation: I surrender all outcomes
to the Divine, and I manifest my dreams.

❉

Now that you have an idea of what is required to help manifest your desires, here are three manifestation tools to help you along the way.

Three Manifestation Tools

Let's face it—when you're trying to manifest your dreams, every bit of assistance counts. When you're deliberately creating your future, you need to call upon every available resource and use every trick in the book to increase your chances for success. Here are three of my favorite manifestation tools to amplify the power behind your thoughts.

Manifestation Numbers

The numbers 1, 8, and 11 are powerful manifestation numbers, so when you're under the influence of a 1, 8, or 11 vibration, you increase your ability to turn your dreams into reality. When you're in a 1, 8, or 11/2 Personal Day, Month, Year, Essence, Pinnacle, or Major Life Cycle Number, or if you have a 1, 8, or 11/2 among your Core Numbers, put extra effort into actualizing your dreams by focusing on what you *want*. But remember, this critical time of manifestation works both ways, and you can easily manifest what you *don't* want simply by giving it your attention. During a cycle of 1, 8, and 11, amplify your positive intentions and minimize your fears.

Clear Quartz Crystal

Holding a piece of clear quartz crystal during visualization will enhance the creative power of your thoughts, which is extremely beneficial to the manifestation process. What's more, clear quartz crystal has a "memory" and can be programmed with your goals and desires. It's a magical healing tool that can help release negative thought patterns, too. If you have low self-esteem, clear quartz can help you build your confidence, especially when it's combined with rose quartz. So wear a piece around your neck, inside your pocket (or bra, if you're a woman), or as a bracelet or ring.

Moon Cycles

Whether you realize it or not, you're closely governed by the cycles of the moon, and certain moon cycles are of great benefit to the manifestation process. The *new moon* is known as the birthing cycle, and is a time to get clear about what you want and then set the intention to get it. This is a powerful time to create a wish list, establish a plan of attack, and leave the rest to the Universe. The new moon cycle is also a time to focus on self-improvement, healing, and reprogramming the limiting beliefs that are holding you back.

When the moon is more visible, it increases in psychic energy; therefore, a *full moon* cycle is the most powerful time to manifest your dreams. By taking action during a full moon cycle, you'll amplify your ability to actualize your dreams. If you want to give your desires their greatest chance of success, set your intention during a *new* moon, then go out there and make it happen during the *full* moon.

For further information about manifestation and the Law of Attraction, I strongly recommend the work of Esther and Jerry Hicks (The Teachings of Abraham®) and Sandra Anne Taylor (*Secrets of Attraction*).

261

✳

Now, let's take a look at recurring numbers.

Recurring Numbers

Sometimes the Universe and angels send you messages in the form of recurring numbers, and when these messages are acknowledged and adhered to, they can improve your quality of life. As you go through your day-to-day activities, you may see a number or sequence of numbers continually appearing on a clock, watch, computer screen, cell phone, license plate, or shopping receipt . . . or even in your dreams! Repetitive numbers can appear anywhere, and the possibilities are endless. Although it may astound or even frighten you at the time, it's important to investigate what the numbers could mean, because nothing is more beneficial than insight "from above."

In numerology, each number has a variety of meanings, so there are several possibilities as to what the exact message of a number, or sequence of numbers, could be. This is where your intuition and common sense are required, because only through honest self-examination and evaluation can you possibly determine the meaning. Because *a number has the same meaning wherever it appears,* this applies to recurring numbers, too. Here is some information on what your recurring numbers could mean.

Recurring Number Meanings

Recurring 1s

Create a new beginning; start something new; leave the past behind; be courageous and strong; embrace your independence; break away from the pack; walk your own path; embrace your individuality; put your creative talents to good use; *you* create what you think—so watch your thoughts at all times; focus your attention on what you *want* rather than what you *don't want;* take action; be proactive.

Recurring 2s

Cooperate with others; be diplomatic; heal your unresolved emotions; love yourself; work on your relationships; embrace a romantic relationship that may be coming into your life; begin a partnership; heal others; heal yourself; create balance in your life; learn to say no; promote harmony; embrace your femininity or feminine side; trust your intuition; develop your psychic abilities.

Recurring 3s

Express yourself creatively; have more fun; be joyous; spend more time with friends; be more social; take up a new hobby; be honest; speak your truth; communicate with others; express your emotions in a healthy way; put your feelings into words; write or journal; be mindful of gossip, criticism, and complaining; see the world through the eyes of a child; spend time with children; take a vacation; work with the ascended masters.

Recurring 4s

Ground yourself; create more stability in your life; be disciplined; work hard; don't give up; put your ideas into physical form; save your money; take your responsibilities seriously; be honest; do the right thing; make a commitment; start building a foundation for your future; persist and persevere; focus on your health; spend more time in nature and the outdoors; know that the angels are around you.

Recurring 5s

Prepare for change; make positive changes; be flexible and adaptable; go with the flow; break free from restraints; be adventurous; experience life; meet new people; try new things; be progressive; think outside the box; be resourceful; travel; go on vacation; exercise temperance and moderation; communicate your thoughts and ideas; promote yourself; take a risk; follow your passion.

Recurring 6s

Know that love is on its way; put effort into your relationships; spend more quality time with your children; be there for your family and friends; work through your family issues; nurture those in need; love yourself; focus on your health; beautify your life and home; get a makeover; heal others; heal yourself; take your responsibilities seriously; leave an unhealthy relationship; start a family; prepare for a baby on the way.

Recurring 7s

Spend quiet time alone; pray regularly; take up yoga, qigong, and/or meditation; discover the secrets and mysteries of the Universe; focus on your health; explore alternative therapies; study metaphysics; focus on your personal or spiritual development; connect with Spirit; discover your spiritual truth; read and do research; go back to school; specialize in something; master your craft; teach others; travel; spend time in nature and the outdoors (especially in or near water).

Recurring 8s

Budget your finances; deal with outstanding debts and legal matters; focus on your career; change your job; consider self-employment; watch your thoughts at all times; be positive; adopt an attitude of abundance; know that your finances will improve; balance the material and spiritual worlds; reclaim your personal power; rise above your ego; accept the recognition that is coming your way; be assured that justice will be served.

Recurring 9s

Prepare for endings and completion, as this is a time of transformation; let go of the things that no longer serve you; trust and surrender; be tolerant; open your mind; forgive yourself and others; heal issues from the past; resolve outstanding conflicts; heal your relationships with family; be compassionate; give selflessly to others; follow humanitarian, animal-related, or environmental pursuits; express yourself creatively; explore the arts.

✳

In the case of recurring number combinations—for example, 645 or 48—the message will be a combination of each individual number's themes. For example, 645 could mean: love is on its way (6) once you create stability in your life (4) and make positive changes (5).

Because the Law of Attraction enables you to attract what you give your attention to, it is also possible to attract recurring numbers into your life simply by focusing on them. With that being said, regardless of whether you *attracted* them or they were sent from the higher realms, recurring numbers can guide you in your life.

For further information about recurring numbers and messages from the angels, I highly recommend Doreen Virtue's book *Angel Numbers 101.*

✦ ✦ ✦

AFTERWORD

Congratulations, my friend! You've made it to the end of this book and are now a numerologist in training. With this greater understanding of yourself, others, and the world around you, the possibilities are endless! Now that you are more aware of your destiny and have glimpsed what lies ahead, you can begin to reach your full potential and make your dreams come true. Hey, you know you can do it—you've seen it in your numbers! So live it, breathe it, be it—*be the best you can be.*

As you harmonize with the energy flow of your numbers, you can navigate your way through life with greater understanding and ease. With this newfound insight and wisdom, you're one step ahead of the game and have everything you need to create a better life.

The ancient wisdom of numerology will not only help you in your own life; it will help you understand and improve others' lives as well. Wisdom is power, and now you've inherited the power to heal through understanding. Be sure to use what you've learned to empower and inspire others wherever you can. When you seek to serve the greater good, the Universe will send you plenty of opportunities to serve.

Whether you use numerology for work or pleasure, you must be diplomatic, compassionate, and positive when relaying sensitive information. This is a responsibility that must be taken seriously—especially when revealing others' challenges, life lessons, and shortcomings. When conducting a reading, be mindful of what you say and how you say it, as some people will take you literally and revolve their lives around your every word. Even though numerology is an ancient tool of divination, no form of forecasting or prediction can be 100 percent correct. So don't claim to know all the answers or make promises you can't keep.

Now that we've come to the end of our journey together, I'd like to take this opportunity to thank you from the bottom of my heart for sharing this wondrous experience with me. Thank you for allowing me to share my wisdom and passion, and thank you for your time. I get very excited when I know that the wisdom of numerology continues to live on in someone's heart, so thank you for taking an interest in the "numbers" and for allowing me the honor of teaching you.

I understand that there's a lot of information to take in, and it can be overwhelming and confusing trying to put it all together. But don't worry—Rome wasn't built in a day. Just take it slowly and absorb what you can gradually. Mastering numerology can take many years, so pace yourself and take your time, practice on yourself and your friends, and be kind to yourself along the way.

Now just before I finish, please allow me to digress from numerology just a little to introduce you to a phenomenal documentary called *Thrive: What on Earth Will It Take?* that's been taking the world by storm (www.thrivemovement.com). If you take pride in making the world a better place, I ask that you please take two hours out of your busy life to watch this enlightening documentary.

Collectively, we can create a massive shift for the betterment of humankind; however, it has to begin with *public awareness*. Not unlike numerology, *Thrive* is one tool to help raise awareness that can institute a positive change. If you see yourself as an ambassador of planet Earth and wish to play a pivotal role in creating a better world, watching this documentary is the perfect place to start. Information is power, and when you're informed—whether by reading a book on numerology or watching a documentary— you're well and truly empowered.

Well, that's all from me, folks. I guess I'd better love you and leave you.

May your life be joyous and abundant, and may all your dreams come true!

Love and blessings,
Michelle

✦ ✦ ✦

GLOSSARY

Birth Day Number: The numerical day of a birth date; indicates special talents and abilities that will assist you on your life path toward fulfilling your destiny; considered by some to have the greatest influence over the middle years of your life, while others believe it reveals your personality strengths and challenges.

Calendar Day Number: The number associated with the calendar day of the month.

Calendar Month Number: The number associated with the calendar month.

Calendar Year Number: The number associated with the calendar year.

Challenges / Challenge Numbers: Calculated from the month, day, and year of your birth date; identify four specific Challenges that must be overcome in order for you to reach your full potential; represent the lessons you must learn to expand your awareness and improve your quality of life. Each Challenge Number runs in conjunction with its accompanying Pinnacle Number.

Core Numbers: The seven numbers that have the most significance with respect to your personality, future potential, and life's journey: Life Path Number, Destiny Number, Soul Number, Personality Number, Maturity Number, Birth Day Number, and Current Name Number.

Cornerstone Number: The first letter of your first name. This number reveals your attitude toward life and how you perceive the world around you.

Current Name Number: Calculated from the first and last name used on a daily basis; has a major influence on your life because it offers additional traits, strengths, lessons, experiences, and opportunities to assist you on your journey, works alongside your existing Destiny Number rather than replaces it.

Cycle of Maturity: *See* Second Major Life Cycle Number.

Cycle of Wisdom: *See* Third Major Life Cycle Number.

Cycle of Youth: *See* First Major Life Cycle Number.

Destiny Number: Calculated from the full original birth-certificate name; the second-most-significant number in your numerology chart, reveals your mission in this life and what you're destined to accomplish; tells you what you'll be most successful doing and reveals one of the several areas of your life that must be developed in order for you to reach your full potential. Combined with the Life Path Number, this is the number to take into consideration when making career choices; also considered by some to represent the accumulation of your past-life achievements.

Essence Number: The sum total of the Physical, Mental, and Spiritual Transits during any given year; a very important number that works in conjunction with the Personal Year Number. It runs from birthday to birthday and provides additional insight into what can be expected for the year; reveals your internal environment, such as your mind-set, needs, desires, and perspectives.

First Challenge Number: Month of birth minus day of birth (or find the difference by subtracting the smaller number from the larger).

First Challenge Period: From birth (age 0) until the age of your Life Path Number subtracted from 36.

First Major Life Cycle Number: The number of your birth month; influences the first 25 to 35 years of your life; governs your formative years; a period of learning and self-discovery.

First Major Life Cycle Period: There are differing opinions among numerologists as to when this period is; either birth to 28 years, birth until the age of transition from the First to the Second Pinnacle Number, or a period calculated from your Life Path Number.

First Name Number: The total of your first name, uncovers additional personality traits and tendencies to assist you on your path.

First Pinnacle Number: Month of birth + day of birth; focuses on self-discovery and realization.

First Pinnacle Period: From birth (age 0) until the age of your Life Path Number subtracted from 36.

Formative Cycle: *See* First Major Life Cycle Number.

Fourth Challenge Number: Month of birth minus year of birth (or find the difference by subtracting the smaller number from the larger).

Fourth Challenge Period: Starts where the third period ends and continues until the end of your life.

Fourth Pinnacle Number: Month of birth + year of birth; focuses on reflection, wisdom, and self-mastery.

Fourth Pinnacle Period: Starts where the third period ends and continues until the end of your life.

Harvest Cycle: *See* Third Major Life Cycle Number.

House Number: Calculated by adding all of the mailbox numbers together and then reducing them to a single-digit number; relates directly to the house and reveals what inhabitants can expect while living there.

Karmic Debt Numbers: 13/4, 14/5, 16/7, or 19/1; indicate particular lessons that failed to be learned in previous lives and which must be mastered in this lifetime; can also indicate the abuse of a particular gift or position of power in a previous life; each has its own unique lessons and burdens.

Karmic Lesson Numbers: Calculated from the missing numbers in a birth-certificate name; indicate weaknesses, along with the specific areas in need of growth that must be addressed in this life.

Last Name Number: The total of your last name; represents the inherited ancestral traits of the family.

Life Path Number: Calculated from your birth date; the most significant number in your numerology chart; reveals the path you've chosen to walk in this life and the lessons you've chosen to master on your journey.

Major Life Cycles: Three blocks of time that highlight the three stages of growth throughout your life.

Major Life Cycle Number: Calculated from the month, day, and year of a birth date; the number associated with a particular Major Life Cycle.

Master Numbers: 11/2, 22/4, and 33/6; higher-octave vibrations of the lower base numbers, 2, 4, and 6; indicate great potential to attain self-mastery during the course of this life; potent energies vibrating at higher frequencies, and their recipients must overcome the lower tendencies of their base numbers before they can fully harness and utilize the powerful force of the Master Number energy.

Maturity Number: Calculated by adding the Life Path Number and Destiny Number together; reveals your future potential and the ultimate goal of your life. Kicks in at maturity or midlife, when you have gained a better understanding of yourself and your life.

Mental Transit: Applies to the letters in your middle name(s); influences your mind-set and the mental aspects of your life.

Numerology: The ancient science of numbers, with each number contributing a unique vibration to the story of your life; can uncover your destiny, life purpose, and future potential, as well as the life lessons you'll face along the way.

Numerology Chart/Profile: A complete chart/profile of your personality and cycle numbers.

Personal Day Number: Calculated by adding the Personal Month Number and Calendar Day Number together; reveals the influence of the day.

Personal Month Number: Calculated by adding the Personal Year Number and Calendar Month Number together; reveals the influence of the month.

Personal Year Cycle: Commences at birth and progresses through nine-year cycles throughout your life; a nine-year cycle of personal growth where each Personal Year Number has a unique theme regarding the types of lessons and experiences you'll encounter for that year.

Personal Year Number: Calculated by adding the month and day of your birth date to the Universal Year Number (calendar year); contains the lessons, opportunities, and experiences you'll encounter during the course of that year. Commences on January 1 and lasts until December 31 or from birthday to birthday, depending on which numerology system you use.

Personality Number: Calculated from the consonants in the birth-certificate name; represents the "outer you," or the side of yourself you're willing to show others; reflects the censored impression you choose to project and the way in which you're perceived by others.

Physical Transit: Applies to the letters in your first name; influences the physical aspects of your life.

Pinnacles: Reveal the atmosphere and events you'll be faced with during each Pinnacle period, along with your potential areas for achievement.

Pinnacle Numbers: Calculated from the month, day, and year of a birth date.

Productive Cycle: *See* Second Major Life Cycle Number.

Recurring Numbers: A number or sequence of numbers continually appearing in your day to day life that are messages from the Universe and angels.

Second Challenge Number: Day of birth minus year of birth (or find the difference by subtracting the smaller number from the larger).

Second Major Life Cycle Number: The number of your birth day; governs your productive years; a period of stabilization and finding your place in the world.

Second Major Life Cycle Period: There are differing opinions among numerologists as to when this period is; either 29–56 years, 27 years from the end of the First Major Life Cycle period, or a period calculated from your Life Path Number.

Second Pinnacle Number: Day of birth + year of birth; focuses on responsibility and relationships with others.

Second Pinnacle Period: Nine years in duration and commences where the first period ends.

Soul Number: Calculated from the vowels in the birth-certificate name; reveals what motivates you and what you need in order to feed your soul.

Spiritual Transit: Applies to the letters in your last name; influences the spiritual aspects of your life.

Street Name Number: Calculated using the same formula to calculate a person's Destiny Number; indicates the energy of the street.

Table of Events Chart: Calculated from your original birth-certificate name; the complete Transit and Essence Number chart of your life.

Third Challenge Number: The difference between the First and Second Challenge Numbers.

Third Challenge Period: Nine years in duration; commences where the second period ends.

Third Major Life Cycle Number: The number of your birth year; influences the remaining years of your life; governs your harvest years; a period of self-empowerment and specialization where your accumulated wisdom and experience enables you to reach your full potential.

Third Major Life Cycle Period: There are differing opinions among numerologists as to when this period is; either from 57 years until the time of passing, from the end of the Second Major Life Cycle period until the time of passing, or a period calculated from your Life Path Number.

Third Pinnacle Number: First Pinnacle Number + Second Pinnacle Number; focuses on maturity and preparation for the fourth and final Pinnacle.

Third Pinnacle Period: Nine years in duration also; commences where the second period ends.

Transits: Each letter of your birth-certificate name, having a specific duration and influence over your life. Together, the Physical, Mental, and Spiritual Transits form the Essence Number.

Universal Day Number: Calculated by adding the Universal Month Number to the Calendar Day Number of inquiry; each has the same meanings as the Personal Day Numbers, except it applies to the world rather than an individual.

Universal Month Number: Calculated by adding the Universal Year Number to the Calendar Month Number of inquiry.

Universal Year Number: The total of the current calendar year; has the same meaning as the Personal Year Number, except it applies to the world rather than an individual.

✦ ✦ ✦

ACKNOWLEDGMENTS

I owe my greatest thanks of all to Louise L. Hay for creating the Hay House empire that has assisted and inspired so many of us in our lives—thank you, Louise! It has been a dream of mine to be a Hay House author for many years, and it is a great privilege and honor to be a part of the Hay House family. Second, I would like to thank Reid Tracy for this wonderful opportunity and for making the biggest dream of my life come true. I'd also like to thank Cheryl Richardson and the "Movers and Shakers: Speak, Write and Promote" workshop for providing such valuable information and for offering all attendees the chance to win a life-changing opportunity.

I'm so lucky to have worked with such an extraordinary team of experts at Hay House! From the bottom of my heart, thank you, Alex Freemon, for holding my hand through the editing and publishing process of my very first book. I'm so grateful you have a number 4! Thank you, Gretel Hakanson, Johanne Mahaffey, and Christy Salinas, for your expertise and guidance. "Cheers" to Duncan Carson and the design team at Hay House UK for creating a book cover I love!

Thank you so very much, Jill Kramer, for your editing expertise and for helping me bring my dream to fruition; you're the best! Thank you, Jonathan Quintin and Evan Mattews, for your creative talent and wisdom. From the bottom of my heart, I would also like to thank you, Ibis Kaba, for believing in me and for discussing your reading with me at dinner. Who would've thought it could've led to this! Donna Abate, Craig Johnson, Nancy Levin, Dr. Wayne Dyer, Serena Dyer, and Karen McCrocklin—thank you for believing in me and for helping me to build my Hay House bridge of friendship. You've each played a valuable part in helping me make my dream come true.

Thank you, Sarah Henry, Vanessa Marshall, and *Woman's Day* magazine, for giving me my very first big break and for letting me contribute to raising the awareness of mainstream New Zealand from 2009 to 2013. Thank you, Brendon Pongia and Sally-Anne Kerr, for the incredible experience of being the resident numerologist for Television New Zealand's *Good Morning*. I'm eternally grateful that you allowed me to share my message with my fellow Kiwis on the big screen. The self-confidence I gained from that experience helped get me to where I am today. You have no idea!

Thank you, my two beautiful children, Ben and Ava, for choosing me to be your mom. I love you very, very much! And thank you, Mom and Dad, Ray and Marilyn Wilson, for loving and supporting me and the kids emotionally, physically, and financially through rocky times. I couldn't have chosen better parents if I tried. Denise Alison—thank you for your friendship and spiritual guidance over the years. You're my spiritual fairy godmother and are definitely part of my soul group. Carole McCarthy—thank you for your intuitive insights and for helping me to see my potential. And to my dear friend Martin Leach, thank you for your humor, friendship, and support when I was a small fish in a big pond with big hopes and dreams.

OMG! Miriam Roberts! Thank you for being my good friend, sounding board, and IT specialist extraordinaire when my IT world comes crashing down. And thank you, Cinna Smith and Matt Aickin, for helping to create a kick-ass "Movers and Shakers" video. Catherine Newton, thank you for encouraging me to dream big back in the day, and thank you, Janice Priest and *Rainbow News,* for the honor of being in your beautiful magazine.

I would also like to take a moment to acknowledge the many numerologists who have gone before me and whose work I have referred to and admired over the years. Thank you: Pythagoras, Juno Jordan, Francie Williams, Hans Decoz, Dan Millman, and David Phillips. Thank you, Joanne Justis, for broadening my understanding of the Chaldean system. I would also like to acknowledge and thank every single person who has been involved in the creation, production, selling, promotion, transportation, and distribution of this book. You're an important link in the chain, and your input is greatly appreciated. If it wasn't for you, my book might not be on the shelves. Thank you! Thank you! Thank you!

Thank you, Archangels Michael and Gabriel, my spirit guides, guardian angels, and loved ones in spirit, for your love, guidance, and protection, and for getting me to this point. And last but certainly by no means least, thank you to everybody who has ever attended one of my workshops or seminars, read my *Woman's Day* column, watched my *Good Morning* segments, listened to my Hay House Radio show, purchased this book or my *Numerology Guidance Cards,* joined my Facebook and Twitter pages, watched one of my YouTube videos, shared one of my Facebook posts, forwarded my monthly forecast, purchased a numerology report, or booked a reading with me. I truly appreciate your time, attention and support because without *you,* I wouldn't be able to do what I love!

+ + +

ABOUT THE AUTHOR

Michelle Buchanan has studied numerology for more than 20 years. She was formerly the spiritual counselor for *Woman's Day* magazine (New Zealand), as well as the resident numerologist for Television New Zealand's *Good Morning*. Michelle has a numerology show, *Numerology Guidance,* on HayHouseRadio.com® and provides personal readings, workshops, and seminars to people all over the world. She is also a talented singer/songwriter and dedicated mother of two based in Auckland, New Zealand.

Website: www.michellebuchanan.co.nz

Hay House Titles of Related Interest

YOU CAN HEAL YOUR LIFE, the movie, starring Louise L. Hay & Friends
(available as a 1-DVD program and an expanded 2-DVD set)
Watch the trailer at: www.LouiseHayMovie.com

THE SHIFT, the movie,
starring Dr. Wayne W. Dyer
(available as a 1-DVD program and an expanded 2-DVD set)
Watch the trailer at: www.DyerMovie.com

ANGEL ASTROLOGY 101: Discover the Angels Connected with Your Birth Chart, by Doreen Virtue and Yasmin Boland (available March 2014)

ANGEL NUMBERS 101: The Meaning of 111, 123, 444, and Other Number Sequences, by Doreen Virtue

ARCHETYPES: A Beginner's Guide to Your Inner-net, by Caroline Myss

COLORS & NUMBERS: Your Personal Guide to Positive Vibrations in Daily Life, by Louise L. Hay

THE COMPLETE BOOK OF NUMEROLOGY: Discovering the Inner Self, by David A. Phillips, Ph.D.

GETTING INTO THE VORTEX: Guided Meditations CD and User Guide, by Esther and Jerry Hicks (The Teachings of Abraham®)

SECRETS OF SUCCESS: The Science and Spirit of Real Prosperity, by Sandra Anne Taylor and Sharon A. Klingler

WHAT COLOR IS YOUR PERSONALITY?: Red, Orange, Yellow, Green . . . , by Carol Ritberger, Ph.D.

YOUR HIDDEN SYMMETRY: How Your Birth Date Reveals the Plan for Your Life, by Jean Haner

All of the above are available at your local bookstore,
or may be ordered by contacting Hay House (see next page).

We hope you enjoyed this Hay House book. If you'd like
to receive our online catalog featuring additional information
on Hay House books and products, or if you'd like to find
out more about the Hay Foundation, please contact:

Hay House, Inc., P.O. Box 5100, Carlsbad, CA 92018-5100
(760) 431-7695 or (800) 654-5126
(760) 431-6948 (fax) or (800) 650-5115 (fax)
www.hayhouse.com® • www.hayfoundation.org

Published and distributed in Australia by: Hay House
Australia Pty. Ltd., 18/36 Ralph St., Alexandria NSW 2015
Phone: 612-9669-4299 • *Fax:* 612-9669-4144 • www.hayhouse.com.au

Published and distributed in the United Kingdom by: Hay House UK, Ltd.,
Astley House, 33 Notting Hill Gate, London W11 3JQ • *Phone:* 44-20-3675-2450
Fax: 44-20-3675-2451 • www.hayhouse.co.uk

Published and distributed in the Republic of South Africa by:
Hay House SA (Pty), Ltd., P.O. Box 990, Witkoppen 2068
Phone/Fax: 27-11-467-8904 • www.hayhouse.co.za

Published in India by: Hay House Publishers India, Muskaan Complex,
Plot No. 3, B-2, Vasant Kunj, New Delhi 110 070 • *Phone:* 91-11-4176-1620
Fax: 91-11-4176-1630 • www.hayhouse.co.in

Distributed in Canada by: Raincoast, 9050 Shaughnessy St.,
Vancouver, B.C. V6P 6E5 • *Phone:* (604) 323-7100 • *Fax:* (604) 323-2600
www.raincoast.com

<u>Take Your Soul on a Vacation</u>

Visit www.HealYourLife.com® to regroup, recharge,
and reconnect with your own magnificence.
Featuring blogs, mind-body-spirit news, and life-changing
wisdom from Louise Hay and friends.

Visit www.HealYourLife.com today!

Simon   10 15 1971 = 25 = (7)

Ed   01 23 1961 = 23 = (5)